CONTENTS

Your Brain and This Book:
A User's Guide

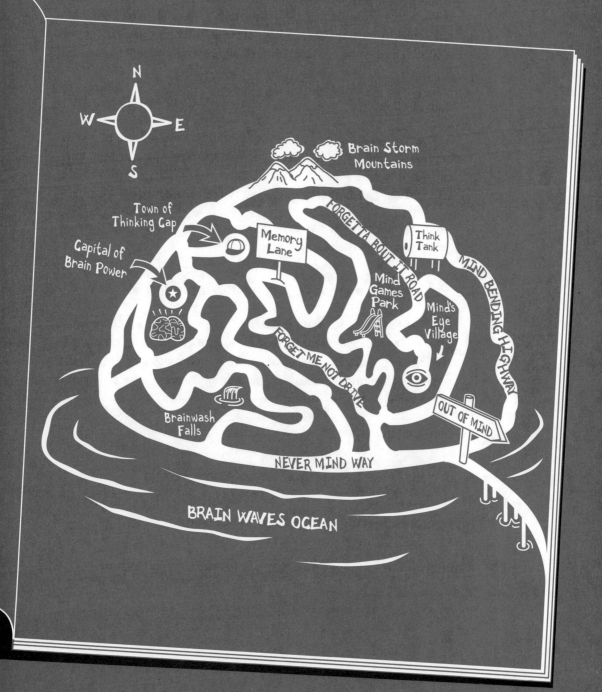

What Is a Mnemonic?

Hmm, *mnemonic* . . . isn't that the weird type of fish your grandma serves the family for Sunday dinners? Or wait, does it have something to do with astronauts and the space shuttle? It's got to be a kind of a sickness, like pneumonia, or a kind of a candy, like nougat. No, I'm sure it's that chemical the park used to clean the algae out of the pool last summer.

Hmm. Or not.

A mnemonic is a memory device. It's something you can use to remember information. It's an effective and powerful tool that has been proven to help people remember names, dates, rules lists, and all types of information. Mnemonics can help you remember *everything!*

There are even mnemonics to help you remember how to spell the word **mnemonic.** Read the sentence below.

▶ **Mary needs easy methods of noting important content.**

The first letter of each word in the sentence spells the word *mnemonic*. Also, the sentence reminds us that using a mnemonic is an easy way to remember content. If you memorize the sentence about Mary, you can remember how to spell *mnemonic* and that mnemonics are simple methods of remembering important information.

Here are some other mnemonics for the word *mnemonic.*

▶ **Mom needs effective methods or nothing is certain!**

▶ **My nanny eats many orange napkins in California.**

▶ **Mannequins never ever mistreat orioles nesting in clothes.**

The great part about mnemonics is that you get to make them up yourself. Sure, we provide hundreds of examples in this book, but some of the best mnemonics are the ones that mean something to you. For example, maybe you can remember how to spell mnemonic by thinking about evil monkeys.

▶ **M**eeting **n**ine **e**vil **m**onkeys **o**n **N**eptune **i**s **c**reepy.

Maybe you can visualize a kind mannequin watching a little bird sleep in a nest of clothes. Or maybe it's easier to imagine a nanny eating orange napkins on the beaches of California. If one of those images sticks with you, you'll be able to better remember how to spell *mnemonic*. Just have fun with the image and let it bounce around in your brain. That's what makes it work!

Everyday Mnemonics

People use mnemonics to remember all sorts of things in their everyday lives.

Farmers use mnemonics to remember how to plant crops. Cooks use mnemonics to remember how to measure ingredients. Carpenters use mnemonics to remember how to use their tools. Doctors use mnemonics to diagnose diseases.

You've even used mnemonics to remember phone numbers, even if you didn't realize it. There are many ways to use mnemonics. There are also many mnemonics that can really save your hide!

▶ Leaves of three, let it be.

You can use this mnemonic when you're camping and need to use some "natural" toilet paper. You wouldn't want to mistakenly use poison ivy. So, this mnemonic can help you pick the best type of leaf to use.

Both the deadly eastern coral snake and the nonpoisonous scarlet king-snake live in the south and southeastern United States. You wouldn't want to mistake a deadly snake for a harmless snake. So, this mnemonic may even save your life!

▶ Red next to yellow could kill a fellow!
Red next to black won't hurt Jack.

You can use this mnemonic below for lots of things: tightening screws, loosening bolts, and opening and closing food jars. You wouldn't want to mistakenly tighten a screw that you were trying to loosen.

▶ Lefty loosey, righty tighty

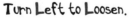

Turn Left to Loosen.   Turn Right to Tighten.

Mnemonics in This Book

There are many different types of mnemonics used by people around the world. We've picked eight of the most common and useful types to include in this book.

ACRONYM

An acronym is a word created using the first letter of each word of the important information. An acronym can also be an abbreviation formed by initial letters.

We use acronyms every day. Here are some examples of commonly used acronyms.

3D: **3**-**d**imensional

DNA: **D**eoxyribo**n**ucleic **A**cid

FAQ: **F**requently **A**sked **Q**uestions

Laser: **L**ight **a**mplification by **s**timulation **e**mission of **r**adiation

NASCAR: **N**ational **A**ssociation for **S**tock **C**ar **A**uto **R**acing

NATO: **N**orth **A**tlantic **T**reaty **O**rganization

Radar: **Ra**dio **d**etection **an**d **r**anging

RAM: **R**andom **A**ccess **M**emory

Scuba: **S**elf-**c**ontained **u**nderwater **b**reathing **a**pparatus

Zip (code): **Z**oning **i**mprovement **p**lan

You can also use acronyms to remember important information for school. Here is an example of an acronym you could use in school.

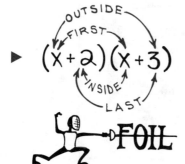

The acronym FOIL can help you remember how to multiply two binomials. If you follow the order First, Outside, Inside, Last, then you won't forget to multiply any of the terms together.

ACROSTIC

An acrostic is a sentence in which the first letter of each word connects with the intended-to-be-recalled information.

Not only can you use acrostics to remember information, but you can also use acrostics to conceal information. For example, if you wanted to write a letter to a friend and conceal a message, you might write the following note.

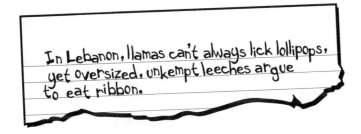

In Lebanon, llamas can't always lick lollipops, yet oversized, unkempt leeches argue to eat ribbon.

Notice how the first letter of each word spells out a hidden message: *I'll call you later.* If your friend knew this code, then your friend would know to expect your phone call.

Here is an example of a commonly used acrostic.

▶ **Eat all dead gophers before Easter.**

This acrostic has been used by people learning to play the guitar as a way to remember the notes of each guitar string: E, A, D, G, B, E, in order from lowest to highest.

Here is an example of an acrostic you could use in school.

▶ **My very energetic mother just served us nine pizzas.**

You can use this acrostic to remember the order of the planets from the sun: Mercury, Venus, Earth, Mars, Jupiter, Saturn, Uranus, Neptune, and Pluto. You may have heard of similar acrostics, such as "My very eager mother just served us nine pickles." Whether it's easier for you to remember pizza, pickles, or pumpernickel, feel free to change any of the mnemonics you find in this book to make them work for you. For more information about the order of the planets, see page 208.

CHAINING

Chaining is a way to link bits of information by making associations between them. With chaining, you visualize a series of connected images or develop a story to connect terms.

You can use chaining to remember a list of chores to do, steps to follow in a project, people to call, items to buy at the grocery store, or other things. Here is an example of chaining.

Grocery List

I had a dream last night in which a lot of **eggs** made their home inside a **milk** carton. They built their beds with slices of **bread**. And their pillows were made with **cheese**. In the backyard of their little home, they had a creek flowing with **orange juice.**

Notice how this story describes strangely memorable images that include eggs, milk, bread, cheese, and orange juice. By recalling this unusual story, you could remember what to buy at the grocery store.

You can also use chaining to remember important information for school. Here is an example of a chaining mnemonic you could use in school.

▶ That crazy **weather**man said the temperature would **cool** down this week, but by Saturday, the **heat** was so intense that we could **melt** a candy bar on the **cement** in seven minutes!

Rocks are formed from other rocks. The different factors in a rock's environment cause one type of rock to change into another type of rock. This is known as the rock cycle. There are five different processes in the rock cycle. The highlighted words in the chaining mnemonic represent these five processes: **weathering, cooling, heat, melting,** and **cementation.**

CHUNKING

Chunking is another way to link information using associations. With chunking, you group related information into smaller, more-manageable categories.

Many people believe that humans can easily recall around seven different things or so at once. So, if you have a list of 20 facts to remember, you may be better able to remember them if you *chunk* the facts into seven groups (or less).

For example, we use chunking all the time to remember phone numbers. Most phone numbers (with area code) have 10 digits. This can be hard to remember, so we use parentheses and dashes to chunk a phone number into three parts: the area code, the first set of three digits (called the exchange), and the next set of four digits. So, instead of trying to remember 3475559122, we can remember (347) 555-9122.

Try this out for fun! Say 10 numbers to a friend and ask your friend to repeat the numbers. Then, say 10 numbers to your friend, but say the numbers as you would a phone number (pause after the third number and after the sixth number). Most likely, your friend will have an easier time correctly remembering the second set of 10 numbers. The same principle applies to your nine-digit social security number.

You can also use chunking to remember important information for school. You can help yourself remember the eight main parts of the human ear by chunking the information into the three categories shown below.

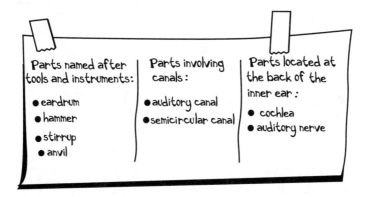

Parts named after tools and instruments:
- eardrum
- hammer
- stirrup
- anvil

Parts involving canals:
- auditory canal
- semicircular canal

Parts located at the back of the inner ear:
- cochlea
- auditory nerve

For more information about the parts of the ear, see page 204.

KEYWORDS

A keyword is a familiar word that sounds like the word or information you need to remember. You've probably used keywords to help remember people's names. If not, you should try it! It's a great way to keep track of names.

For example, let's say you meet a girl named Madeleine. The first time you meet her, you can form a mental image of her going *mad*. Then, every time you see her, you can remember the image, which will help you remember her name!

▶ The name **Madeleine** begins with the word **mad**.

How about if you met a boy named Frank? Perhaps you could form a mental image of him eating a *frank*furter—or even having a hot dog for a head! Then, every time you see him, you can associate him with the image, which will help you remember his name!

▶ The name **Frank** sounds like **frankfurter**.

Give it a try. Part of the goal of this book is to show you how to make up your own mnemonics when there's something you need to remember. To get some practice, pick a friend or family member and come up with a keyword that could help a stranger remember that person's name.

You can also use keywords to remember important information for school. Here's an example for U.S. History.

Manifest Destiny was the nineteenth-century belief that the United States was destined to take over all the land west to the Pacific Ocean. The keyword *feast* sounds like *–fest,* and you can eat greedily and take all the food you want in a feast. You can use this keyword mnemonic to remember that people who believed in Manifest Destiny wanted to consume all the land.

▶ "Mani-Feast Destiny"

For more information about Manifest Destiny, see page 93.

THE LOCI METHOD

The loci method is one of the oldest known memory techniques. The word *loci* means *places,* and the loci method is an association of familiar places with information. For example, you might place certain information at certain spots in your room, house, neighborhood, or an imaginary place. Then, you can observe the details of each place or landmark as you follow a path, whether mentally or physically, remembering the information in the correct order.

You've probably used the loci method to find something that you've lost. Consider this example of the loci method.

Jordan had a great day with friends, but he lost his watch. He recalls the day's activities and decides to retrace all his steps to find the watch.

First, Jordan left home and walked to the park to meet his friends. They sat on the swings for a little while. Next, they went to a music store and looked at CDs. After that, they all went to the local ice cream place. Jordan still had his watch on because he remembered checking the time. Finally, Jordan walked home and checked the mailbox before going inside. He got a birthday card from his aunt, which he put in his pocket.

By retracing his steps during the day, Jordan was able to use the loci method to find his missing watch. He realized it must have fallen off in the mailbox.

You can also use the loci method to remember important information for school. For example, you will be expected to know the properties of waves.

Waves have different properties. The **crest** of a wave is the highest point of a wave. It is the maximum distance upward from the rest position. The **trough** of a wave is the lowest point of a wave. It is the maximum distance downward from the rest position. The **wavelength** is the distance between successive crests or successive troughs. **Frequency** describes the number of wavelengths occurring in a given unit of time. **Amplitude** usually describes the height of a wave, or the distance from the rest position to the crest or the trough.

The Properties of Waves

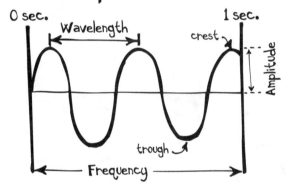

▶ Write the words *crest*, *trough*, *wavelength*, *frequency*, and *amplitude* on index cards. Then, walk around your home and put the cards in places where they can help you remember the meaning of the property.

First, tape the crest card to your bedroom ceiling because that is the highest point in your room. Next, place the trough card on the floor, the lowest point in the room. Put the wavelength card near a ruler because you use a ruler to measure distance. Then, place the frequency card near a calendar because a calendar represents time. Finally, put the amplitude card on the bed because that is where you take a rest.

If you were taking a test in science class that asked you to define *trough* you could remember that the trough card was on your bedroom floor, which would remind you that the trough must be the lowest point of a wave. You'll be surprised by how powerful the loci technique can be.

PEGWORD

A pegword is a short word that rhymes with a specific number and is easy to visualize. You can also develop your own pegwords. To use this type of mnemonic, you must learn the pegwords and the numbers with which they rhyme.

These are the pegwords we have used in this book. Notice how the number rhymes with its accompanying pegword.

One = Bun   Two = Shoes   Three = Tree   Four = Door

Five = Hive   Six = Sticks   Seven = Heaven

A pegword mnemonic helps us remember things in the correct order. Sometimes, we need to remember events or steps in order. You simply need to choose an image to represent each thing you want to remember, and then tie that image together with the correct pegword. For example, if you need to remember the first step in a process, you would come up with a mental picture that combined that step with a bun.

You can use pegwords if you need to remember a list that includes more than seven things. Just come up with pegwords that rhyme with *eight, nine,* and *ten.* Here are some examples.

Eight	Nine	Ten
bait	bovine	pen
classmate	clothesline	den
crate	porcupine	firemen
skate	swine	pigpen

You can use a pegword mnemonic in your everyday life. For example, you might use pegwords to remember your class schedule because pegwords are helpful when you have to remember things in a specific order. Look at this example that shows you how a student could use pegwords to remember his or her first three classes.

Period	Class
1	English
2	Math
3	Science
4	Gym
5	Lunch
6	Art
7	History
8	Spanish

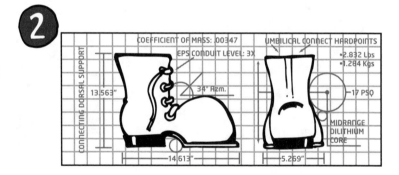

You can also use the pegword method to remember important information for school. For example, you may study P. T. Barnum in history class. Three of his major achievements, in chronological order, were opening the American Museum in Manhattan, touring with a famous opera singer known as the Swedish Songbird, and founding "The Greatest Show on Earth," the circus.

You can use the pegword method to remember P. T. Barnum's three major achievements using pegwords. See below.

▶ The pegword for one is *bun*, so the bun displayed on the pedestal can help you remember that opening the American Museum was Barnum's first act.

The pegword for two is *shoe*, so the shoe with a songbird living inside can help you remember that touring with the Swedish songbird was Barnum's second act.

The pegword for three is *tree*, so the tree growing through the circus tent can help you remember that starting the circus was Barnum's third act.

RHYMING MNEMONIC

A rhyming mnemonic is a catchy verse that includes important information and rhymes. Rhyming is an incredibly helpful way to remember stuff. For example, the jingles in an advertisement often rhyme because the rhyme will stick in your head, helping you remember the product.

Even before people used written language, rhyming songs about historical events were used to pass on information. The rhyme helped the singers remember their songs and thus the stories.

Here are some examples of everyday rhyming mnemonics.

▶ Lefty loosey, righty tighty

We use this to remember which way to turn screws, nuts, lids, and lightbulbs.

▶ Thirty days have September, April, June, and November.
All the rest have thirty-one, except February, which has twenty-eight, and in leap year twenty-nine.

This mnemonic rhymes in the first sentence. In addition, it has rhythm. We use this to remember the number of days in each month of the year.

▶ Red sky at night: shepherd's delight.
Red sky in morning: shepherd's warning.

The words *night* and *delight* rhyme, and the words *morning* and *warning* rhyme, making the mnemonic memorable. This mnemonic tells us that a red sky at night may show that the weather will be pleasant, but a red sky in the morning may mean that there will be storms.

You can also use rhyming to remember important information for school. Here are examples of rhyming mnemonics you could use in school.

▶ It's *i* before *e,* except after *c,*
or when it sounds like "ay"
as in *neighbor* or *weigh.*
(And *weird* is weird.)

> You can use rhyming to remember spelling rules. For more information about spelling words with *i* and *e,* see page 41.

▶ **S**even **s**potted **s**wans **s**at **s**peaking in the **s**un,
using words with first letter repetition.
"What are these **s**imilar **s**tarting **s**ounds?" asked one.
"My **f**eathered **f**riend, it's alliteration."

> You can use rhyming to remember the meaning of the word *alliteration.* For more information about alliteration, see page 74.

▶ You can add fractions that have the same bottom;
Then only the top numbers sum.
You can multiply fractions any old time—
top times top and bottom times bottom.

> See! You can even use rhyming to remember how to add and multiply fractions! For more information about adding fractions, see page 152.

Figuring Out How You Learn Best

When we learn, we use our mind and our body. We use our body when we use our senses of sight, sound, taste, touch, and smell. We also use our body when we move. Some people prefer to study alone in a quiet environment, seated at a chair. Others might prefer to study in a group with lots of conversation, or while pacing around a room.

Do you know how you like to learn?

Try to figure out what methods of learning work best for you. Think about a time when you've succeeded at school, at home, or with a hobby. Remember how you learned what you needed to succeed. Knowing how you learn best can help you make the most of your natural strengths.

Imagine that your teacher told you to learn about the Andes Mountains. If you could learn any way you wanted, how would you want to learn?

KINESTHETICALLY

When you learn kinesthetically, you use your sense of touch or body movement. You may learn best by moving around or acting something out.

Would you get a plane ticket to the Andes Mountains, would you hike a nearby mountain, or would you pace your room as you studied what you were reading?

VISUALLY

When you learn visually, you use your sense of sight. You may learn best by looking at pictures, outlines, or maps. You may like to draw pictures to help you learn. You need to use your sense of sight to read and write too.

Would you run to the library and read books about the Andes Mountains, draw a picture of the Andes Mountains, or go online to look at photographs of the mountains?

Auditorily

When you learn auditorily, you use your sense of sound. You may learn best by listening to your teacher speak, discussing with friends and classmates, and listening to music while you study. You may like to tap a rhythm with your pen or pencil while you study.

Would you go online to download a lecture about the Andes Mountains or discuss the Andes Mountains with someone who knows about them?

Or would you use a combination of these methods? Using multiple methods of learning can often reinforce the information you're trying to retain, so don't be afraid to try learning in different ways.

Once you know how you like to learn, you can plan how you study. You can make sure you use learning methods that work for you when you study for important tests.

Using the Learning Tips

Throughout the book, you'll find kinesthetic tips, audio tips, and visual tips. There are tips for each mnemonic. You can use these tips to help you learn and remember the information that's provided.

You can use what you know about how you like to learn with these tips. You may find that some tips match your learning strengths, while you may choose not to follow others. Don't hesitate to come up with your own tips, too, depending on the types of learning that you prefer.

In addition to the learning tips, you will also find two additional features called "It's Your Turn" and "Get This." These features provide interesting information about memory techniques and allow you to test your memory.

Consider these examples of kinesthetic, audio, and visual tips for English Language Arts concepts.

KINESTHETIC TIP

As you read this page, stomp your foot every time you come to a period that ends a sentence. Then, pick up any book or magazine and do the same thing. This will emphasize the primary function of periods, which is to create pauses, or breaks, in a text.

Each kinesthetic tip gives you a way to use your sense of touch or body movement to develop your memory of the information in the accompanying mnemonic. For example, acting out the action for the mnemonic may help you recall the subject matter.

AUDIO TIP

Think of examples of onomatopoeia. Say the words aloud dramatically, making them sound the way the actual sounds do. Mimic the sharp "crack" of a baseball bat. Imitate the menacing "hiss" of a slithering snake. See if you can recreate the "pop" of a balloon bursting.

Each audio tip guides you to use your sense of sound to develop your memory of the information in the accompanying mnemonic. For example, singing or clapping along to a mnemonic may cement the information in your brain.

VISUAL TIP

Draw a silly picture that shows a literal interpretation of a simile. For example, maybe you hear the same annoying pop song on the radio every day and you can't get the tune out of your head. You could say, "That catchy song is like bubble gum that's stuck to my brain." Of course you wouldn't mean it literally. But if you did, what would it look like? This will help you remember the meaning of a simile.

Each visual tip provides ways to use your sense of sight to develop your memory of the information in the accompanying mnemonic. For example, looking at images may strengthen your memory of the information.

Consider these examples of the "It's Your Turn" and "Get This" features.

"IT'S YOUR TURN" TIP

Each "It's Your Turn" tip guides you to get connected and involved with your memory and how you learn. An "It's Your Turn" tip may encourage you to come up with your own unique mnemonic to remember the content, or it may allow you to test your own memory.

IT'S YOUR TURN

Think of a class you have in school that has assigned seating. Try listing every student in the class based on the order in which their desks are arranged. Start with the person in the back left of the room and move right, or start with your own seat and move outward. See how long it takes you to name everyone using this technique, and check to make sure you didn't leave anyone off of the list. You're using the loci technique!

"GET THIS . . ." TIP

Each "Get This" tip provides you with fun, weird facts or anecdotes about the accompanying mnemonic or memory technique.

66 Get This . . .

Did you know that some people consider the sea surrounding Antarctica to be the world's fifth ocean? This body of water has long been differentiated by mariners as the Southern Ocean because of its distinct currents. In 2000, the International Hydrographic Organization officially recognized the Southern Ocean, although many organizations still disagree with this definition. 99

Memory Helpers

In 1940, the average twenty-five-year-old adult in the United States had completed about eight years of schooling. In 2004, the average 25-year-old adult in the United States had completed about thirteen years of schooling. That's a lot more information to hold in your brain! But there's some good news!

Once you have truly understood a piece of information, it gets stored in your brain and it doesn't go anywhere. You just need to know how to access it. Your brain is the greatest tool in the world when you can help it store and retrieve information.

Here are some memory helpers for understanding, retaining, and recalling information better.

- **Be interested.** When you are truly interested in the content, you learn better and remember information more easily. If you don't find something interesting, try to make it interesting. Try to think of ways to change the mnemonics in this book to make them more interesting—and more memorable.

- **Be picky.** Identify the most important bits of information to remember. You can do this by reading the titles and headings of sections of a book. You can skim sections too. Then, you can pick out what information is most essential to remember. You've probably done this before when you've highlighted a book, but the more attention you can give the most critical details, the better off you'll be.

- **Use your senses.** You can strengthen your memory of information by using your senses while you study. Try to involve your senses of sight, sound, taste, touch, and smell. Get moving when you study too. Make sure to involve your senses in ways that will support your learning and your ability to remember.

- **Make connections.** Connect with what you are learning by thinking deeply about the content and by asking questions. Consider how the information connects with your life, your experiences, and what you already know. Make the information meaningful to you.

- **Review.** Reviewing information often is essential to retaining knowledge. Try studying in short bursts so that you don't drain your energy. Review your notes before and after classes. And be sure to practice, practice, practice.

As you read the mnemonics in this book, think about how you can make them more memorable. Mnemonics are only as good as you make them. No matter what, make sure the mnemonics are useful to you. Ask yourself the following questions:

- Am I interested?
- Am I focusing on the most important information?
- Am I using my senses?
- Am I making connections?
- Have I reviewed and practiced?

Ready for a Challenge?

People around the world pit their memories against each other for prizes, glory, and the right to be dubbed the "Grandmaster of Memory."

ORGANIZATIONS

You can find out more about memory organizations by visiting these Web sites:

- Check out the World Memory Sports Council. Many countries are a part of the World Memory Sports Council, including the United Kingdom, Canada, China, Germany, Mexico, the United States of America, and others.

  www.worldmemorychampionship.com

- The United States of America is a member of the World Memory Sports Council. Visit the USA National Memory Championship's Web site for information about memory sports in the United States.

  www.usamemoriad.com

- The UK Memory Sports Council is a member of the World Memory Sports Council. Check out the UK Memory Sports Council for information about memory sports in the United Kingdom.

  www.memoryengland.com

COMPETITIONS

Memory competitions occur around the world. These competitions are like the Olympics for the mind, and they test the limits of human memory. People of all ages and nationalities compete with each other. Competitors are asked to memorize a series of numbers, a series of playing cards, a poem, random words, and other information.

Since 1991, the World Memory Sports Council has organized an annual World Memory Competition. The winner of this competition is dubbed the "Grandmaster of Memory."

Since 1998, the United States has also organized an annual competition called the U.S.A. Memory Championship. This competition is also called the U.S.A. Memoriad.

If you want to compete in the U.S.A. Memoriad, you have to be at least 12 years old. You can prepare and test yourself with the examples provided at www.usamemoriad.com/Archives/Archives.htm. You can find out more information by going to www.usamemoriad.com/Contact/Contact.htm.

Never be at a loss for words...

The Meaning of *Aghast*

▶ "A-gasped"

The word **aghast** means "struck with terror, amazement, or horror."

The illustration shows a shocked and frightened girl who is gasping. Because someone might gasp when she is feeling aghast, the keyword "a-gasped" will help you remember the meaning of *aghast*.

One good way to memorize a new vocabulary word is to act it out or pronounce it with the emotion it describes. For example, you could hold your hands to your face or shield your eyes and exclaim the word "aghast" as if you were truly horrified. If you do this a couple of times, you're more likely to "program" the meaning of the word into your brain.

❝ *Get This . . .*

The illustration above is a parody of a famous painting by Edvard Munch, called *The Scream*. In August 2004, this valuable painting was stolen from the Munch Museum in Norway. The two armed robbers simply lifted the painting off of the wall and ran out of the museum to their getaway car. Upon hearing this news, people around the world probably made the same face as the subject of the painting, *aghast* that something so terrible could happen to such an important treasure of the art world. ❞

The Meaning of *Orator*

▶ **oral** narra**tor**

An **orator** is a skilled public speaker. You know that a narrator is a storyteller and that the word *oral* means "spoken," so you can use the phrase *oral narrator* to help you remember the definition of *orator*. And not only do *orator* and *oral narrator* sound alike, but the first and last three letters of the keyword phrase spell the word *orator!*

Whom do you consider to be a powerful public speaker? Maybe Martin Luther King Jr. comes to mind as an eloquent orator. Maybe you are thinking of a great politician, such as Abraham Lincoln. Maybe you remember a speaker from an assembly at school or a classmate who made a speech while running for student government. Use the name of this person in a sentence, describing him or her as a good orator. Repeat the sentence aloud.

Examples:

"Dr. King was a famous orator. Everyone has heard of his 'I Have a Dream' speech."

"Lincoln's powerful Gettysburg Address showed that he was a talented orator."

Stand up and pretend you are a noted orator. Imagine someone took a photo of you as you were speaking to a large crowd. What would the photo look like? Would your arms be raised for emphasis? Would you have one hand over your chest to show that you were sincere? Picture yourself speaking to the audience. Then, pose as you would be seen in the photo. Imagine the caption below your photo: "Famous orator [your name here] addresses a standing-room-only crowd."

Homophones

Homophones are words that sound the same, but are spelled differently and have different meanings. The prefix *homo–* means "the same" or "alike" (as in *homogeneous* and *homosexual*). The root *–phone* means "sound" (as in *telephone* or *phonetic*).

In the picture above, the words *ring* and *wring* are homophones. They sound the same, but have different spellings and meanings. A ring is like a hoop or a band, or it is the sound a bell makes. To wring something is to squeeze or twist it, the way you might do with a wet towel.

. . . .

IT'S YOUR TURN

How many homophone pairs can you find in the story below?

Rudolph Mackey was the bizarre heir to a fortune made from condiments. Mackey Mustard was sold in every town fair and bazaar in the nation, and it graced hot dogs all around the world. Although he stood to inherit millions of dollars and cents, there was an air of sadness around this eccentric "Duke of Dijon." His fame made him scared to go out in public, for fear of being chased by the paparazzi. Any time he thought about leaving his mansion, his head reeled and the room whirled. When he mustered up the courage to go out, he went under the guise of a chaste nun. But he was usually sniffed out by the camera guys because of the scents of mustard stains on his suits.

Complement vs. *Compliment*

▶ A **complem**ent **complet**es something.

Many people confuse the words *complement* and *compliment*. The keyword mnemonic reminds you that a **complement** is something that completes or goes together well with something else.

Examples:

Fresh-baked chocolate brownies need the *complement* of a tall glass of cold milk.

The moving lyrics were the perfect *complement* to the beautiful melody.

A **compliment,** on the other hand, is a form of praise, or an admiring remark.

Examples:

I wrote the songwriter a letter of *compliment* on his fine work.

Tara paid her mother a *compliment* on her new hairstyle and then asked to borrow the car.

Use the same mnemonic to remember the difference between the adjective forms, *complementary* and *complimentary*.

Examples:

complementary colors (opposite colors that balance each other)
complimentary comments (admiring remarks)

" Get This . . .

In mathematics, the term *complementary angles* describes two angles whose measures add up to 90 degrees. Consider that the two complementary angles *complete* a right angle, and you'll be spelling properly in your math class too.

(It would be silly to call two angles "complimentary," unless they say things to each other like "You're so a-cute!" Sorry, bad joke.) **"**

Idioms

▶

How to Remember Everything • Grades 6–8

When you hear an idiom, is it *music to your ears*? Does it *ring a bell,* or does it go *over your head*?

An **idiom** is an expression that cannot be understood from the literal definitions of the words. If your new jeans *cost an arm and a leg,* that does not mean you left the mall without two limbs. It means the jeans were expensive. And, if you ask your teacher how she knows you finished your homework during class and she says, *"A little bird told me,"* it doesn't mean that she communicates with pigeons. It means she does not want to tell you how she got the information.

The picture on the previous page shows literal interpretations of several idioms. Have you ever been *in a pickle*? That means you're in some sort of trouble, like the man in the pickle car who's about to drive into a tree! The expression *when pigs fly* means something is probably never going to happen. Picture this scene to remember the meaning of the word *idiom* and a few examples of idioms.

· · · · · · · · · · · ·
IT'S YOUR TURN

Play a game called Idiom Memory with a friend or family member. You will need 20–30 index cards. On each index card, write one of the following words or phrases:

a piece of cake
simple

Break a leg!
Good luck!

elbow grease
hard work

on the dot
right on time

hit the books
study

two-faced
deceitful

give a hand
help out

To create the rest of the idiom cards, come up with your own pairs. Then, put all the cards in a pile, facedown, and shuffle them. Spread them across the table in even rows. The first player will turn over one card, then another card. If those two words are synonyms, that player gets to pick up those cards. If not, it is the next player's turn to try to make an idiom pair. Keep going until all the cards have been picked up: the player with the most cards wins.

The Meaning of *Abridged*

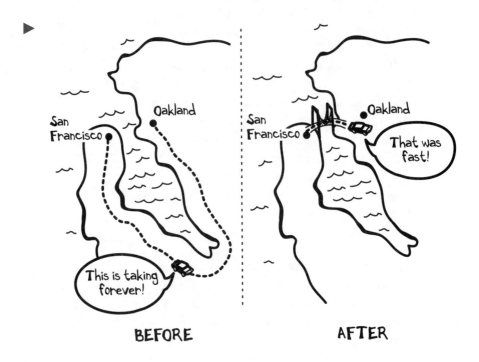

BEFORE   AFTER

The word ***abridged*** means "shortened." Check out the map above, and notice that *a bridge* makes the trip between San Francisco and Oakland much shorter. Without a bridge, the trip between two cities would take a long time because you would have to drive around the water. However, travel across a bridge and the trip will be *abridged*.

The word *abridge* is most often used to describe a text that has been shortened. An *abridged* dictionary is one that omits rarely used words. An *abridged* version of a novel is one that has been shortened to make it easier to read.

❝ *Get This . . .*

The George Washington Bridge, the only bridge that connects Manhattan to New Jersey, abridged the travel time to get from New York to New Jersey when it was opened to traffic in 1931. New Yorkers often refer to the bridge as the GWB—an abridged name for the George Washington Bridge! ❞

The Meaning of *Alienate*

▶ You and your friends have a club. A space alien joined the club along with the rest of your friends. To celebrate your new member, you planned a big party. You bought lots of delicious food. But before the party could take place, the **alien ate** all the food in your clubhouse—including your friend Adam. As a result, you and your friends decided to make a new club rule: Anyone who *eats* another club member will be kicked out of the club.

The word ***alienate*** means "to be unfriendly to" or "to reject from a group." In the story above, the alien was *alienated* from the rest of the group because he ate all the food for the party, not to mention one of the attendees!

Baron vs. Barren

Baron Ron and the Barren Tree

The words *baron* and *barren* are homonyms, which means they sound the same but have different spellings and meanings.

A **baron** is someone who has great power or influence. In Europe, a baron might be a nobleman. In the United States, a baron could be a powerful business tycoon.

The word **barren,** on the other hand, means "producing little or no vegetation." A desert could be considered barren land because very few plants can grow in that climate.

Baron has the name Ron in it. To remember that a baron is a person, picture a powerful man named Ron, like the guy with the crown, flexing his muscles in the picture.

Barren is another form of the adjective *bare*. Land or plants without vegetation are bare. To remember this, imagine the barren apple tree with no apples growing on it.

The Meaning of *Reprieve*

► To postpone a punishment,
or to relieve.
Either way, I sure do hope
for a **reprieve**.

Think of a time when you have been *reprieved* of something. Did your parents reprieve you from being grounded so that you could go to a movie or a concert? Did the rain give you a reprieve from having to mow the lawn?

The word **reprieve** means "to postpone or cancel a punishment." It also means "to provide temporary relief, especially from pain." The rhyme includes both definitions and can help you remember the meaning of *reprieve*.

So, the next time you're stuck in your room with no phone or TV privileges, you might want to chant this rhyme and hope it comes true.

❝ *Get This . . .*

Here's a word you don't hear too often: *lethologica*. It means "an inability to remember the right word." Imagine that you are trying to think of the word that describes those little 3-D models you used to build in elementary school . . . sometimes you had to look through a hole in the box to see the scene . . . it starts with a *d* and it sounds like a nasty stomach upset. Oh yeah, it's *diorama*! Reviewing the vocabulary mnemonics in this book will help ensure that you don't suffer from lethologica in the future. And while you're at it, you might want to create a mnemonic to help you remember what *lethologica* means! ❞

Connotation and Denotation

The **denotation** of a word is its dictionary definition. The **connotation** of a word is its suggested or implied meaning. The connotation can shade a word in such a way that it stirs up certain thoughts or feelings, showing what you *really* mean. For example, *cheap* and *inexpensive* have similar *denotations*—both words mean "costing little." However, *inexpensive* has a more positive connotation, implying that you got a good deal, while the word *cheap* sounds more negative, implying that an item is of low quality.

. . . .
It's Your Turn

The words *slim, scrawny, thin, slender, bony,* and *gaunt* all have similar denotations, but different connotations. *Slim, thin,* and *slender* are more positive descriptions, while *scrawny, bony,* and *gaunt* sound more like insults. Think of other sets of words that have similar denotations. Then, compare the connotations. Which words suggest a more positive image? What are the subtler shades of each word?

The Meaning of *Torrid*

▶ Too red!

The word **torrid** means "extremely hot, or scorching." If the weather is torrid, you will probably be sweating and your face will be red. The color red is often associated with heat or warmth, so the keywords "Too red!" should help you remember the meaning of *torrid*.

Picture a desert scene similar to the one above, with a big red sun. Imagine details that will help you remember "too red." For example, you might be holding a red-hot poker, or there might be a stream of red lava running through the sand. Really try to imagine what it would feel like to be there.

Not many people find torrid weather enjoyable. In fact, most of us think such conditions are horrid. Because *torrid* and *horrid* sound alike, this could be another clue for remembering the definition. *Torrid* also rhymes with *forehead* (almost), so you could imagine being so hot that sweat was dripping from your forehead. Remember that you don't have to use our suggestion—choose a keyword that works for you.

The Meaning of *Tenement*

▶ "ten men"

A **tenement** is a high-rise apartment building in an urban area. These apartments are often inexpensive and house many people, and they barely meet minimum standards of safety.

At the turn of the twentieth century, many poor immigrants in the United States lived in tenements with terrible living conditions. The tiny rooms were usually damp and dark with no air flow or running water. Many neighbors had to share a bathroom and the residents had no privacy. In fact, sometimes an entire extended family lived in one room.

The keywords "ten men" can help you remember that a *tenement* is a building where many people live in cramped conditions.

Picture ten men sleeping in a one-room apartment. Maybe there are five sets of double bunks lined up next to each other. Or maybe there are two big mattresses side by side on the floor and the men are sleeping all in a row. When you think of the ten men sleeping in cramped quarters, you will remember what a tenement is.

Spelling Words with *I* and *E*

▶ It's *i* before *e*, except after *c*,
or when it sounds like "ay"
as in *neighbor* or *weigh*.
(And *weird* is weird.)

You've probably heard at least part of this spelling rhyme before. When a word has the long \e\ sound, such as *piece, niece,* or *believe,* the rule is that *i* comes before *e*.

However, if these letters come immediately after the letter *c* (or an *s* that makes a soft \c\ sound), then *e* comes before *i,* as in *ceiling, receive,* or *seizure.*

Also, *e* comes before *i* if the letters make the long \a\ sound, as in *neighbor, reign,* or *weigh.*

The word *weird* is an exception to the rule. In fact, there are many exceptions to this rule, including *neither, foreign, height, caffeine,* and *heir.* But the rule is still pretty useful.

IT'S YOUR TURN

List as many words as you can in which *i* comes before *e* when the letters appear consecutively. Then, list a bunch of words in which *e* comes before *i* when the letters appear consecutively. Say the words and notice the differences in the vowel sounds.

Imagine that you live next door to Old MacDonald—you know, the guy with the farm. To help you remember the second line of the spelling rhyme, pretend that he is your neighbor. Then, hum the song from your preschool days. "Old MacDonald had a farm, E-I-E-I-O." This will help you remember that to spell words with the "ay" sound heard in *neighbor,* the rule is always "*e* before *i*."

Forming the Past Tense

▶ To form the past tense of a **regular verb**,
add –d or *–ed* to the end of the word.
Irregular verbs follow a different plan,
such as *went, flown, taught,* and *began.*

The past and past participle of **regular verbs** are formed by adding *–d* or *–ed* to the end of the word. For example, the past tense of *believe* is *believed* and the past participle of *cook* is *cooked. Learned, typed, listened,* and *copied* are other examples of regular verbs in the past tense. (Note that the past and past participle are the same for regular verbs, but the past participle is usually preceded by *had, have,* or *has.*)

The past and past participle of **irregular verbs** are formed in ways other than by adding *–d* or *–ed. Begin* is an irregular verb because the past tense is *began* and the past participle is *begun* (instead of *beginned*). Other examples of irregular verbs (in the past or past participle) are *bought, kept, made, sold, thought, seen, bitten,* and *wrote.*

Say the poem without looking. As you perform the poem, alternately pat your legs and snap your fingers on the beat. You can even come up with your own drum solo to go along with the mnemonic. Read it aloud as you pat and snap. Adding the rhythm will help the poem "click" in your mind.

Forming Plurals: When to Add −es

▶ **C**harming **s**urgeons **sh**yly **X**-ray **z**ebras.

Most **plural nouns** are formed simply by adding −*s* to the end of the word. However, there are several exceptions. An exception to the rule involves nouns ending with **ch, s, sh, x,** or **z.** To form the plurals of these words, it is necessary to add −*es*.

Examples:

witches   dishes   blitzes

atlases   foxes

The acrostic can help you remember when to add −*es*. Each word in the mnemonic begins with a letter or letters that can remind you of when to add −*es* to the end of a word.

Think of several examples of words ending in *ch, s, sh, x,* and *z.* Write the words and add −*es* to form the plurals. Read the plurals aloud. Notice that adding −*es* to make a plural adds an extra syllable to the word. This is not true for plurals that are formed simply by adding −*s*. Compare the endings of the words *crutches* and *cards*. There is an extra syllable at the end of *crutches* because we added −*es*. Paying attention to the sounds of these plurals can help you remember when to add −*es* to the end of a word.

Immigrant vs. Emigrant

▶ **E**migrants **e**xit,
Immigrants come **i**n.

People confuse the words *immigrant* and *emigrant* because they sound alike. **Emigrants** are people who exit their home countries. **Immigrants** are people who come into a new country. You can use the words *exit* and *in* to help you remember the difference between emigrants and immigrants. Both *emigrant* and *exit* start with the letter *e,* and both *immigrant* and *in* start with the letter *i*.

Spelling Calendar

▶ There are **two *a*'s** in *calendar*: one for **April**, the other for **August**.

The word ***calendar*** is often misspelled *calender,* with two *e*'s rather than two *a*'s. You can remember that *calendar* has two *a*'s by recognizing that there are two months beginning with the letter *a* in the *calendar*. Those months are, of course, April and August.

While learning this mnemonic, purposely mispronounce the word *calendar* as cah-len-DAHR. Stressing the *–ar* sound at the end of the word will help you remember the proper spelling.

People commonly use mnemonics to help them remember which months have 31 days and which have only 30 (or 28). Many people know the rhyme "30 days have September, April, June, and November." But there is another cool trick that can help you remember the number of days in a month.

Make a fist. Tap your first knuckle and say "January." Because January "lands" on a knuckle, that means January has 31 days. Then, tap the space between your first knuckle and your second knuckle and say "February." February does not fall on a knuckle, so it does *not* have 31 days. Continue through the remaining months. After the last knuckle, July, go back to the beginning and tap your first knuckle for August. That means July and August are consecutive months that have 31 days. Cool trick, huh?

Lose vs. Loose

▶ Add another *o* and you **loosen** up the word.
Take away an *o* and you **lose** letters.

People often confuse the spellings of the words **lose,** which is the opposite of win, and **loose,** which is the opposite of tight. This mnemonic can help you remember that *lose* is spelled with just one *o* and *loose* has an extra *o*.

Imagine that the *o*'s are holes in a belt. If you gain weight, then you might need to loosen up your belt, which means you have to add another hole, or another *o*!

Spelling Noticeable

► **Notice**, if you are **able**, the *e* in *noticeable*.

> ***Noticeable*** is a commonly misspelled word. Often, the letter *e* is left out. To make sure you spell this word correctly, be sure to *notice* the *e*. Also, as the sentence shows, the words *notice* and *able* are both in the word *noticeable*.

> Try writing the word *noticeable* in different ways. Use a red marker to write the first part of the word, *notice*. Then, use a blue marker to write the ending, *able*.

> Also, try writing the entire word, except the *e,* in blue. Then, write the *e* in red to make it stand out. If the *e* is *noticeable,* you will easily remember to include it the next time you write the word.

Capital vs. Capitol

► *Capital* has **a lot** of meanings. *Capitol* has **one** meaning.

> The word ***capital*** refers to several things. For example, it can mean money or material wealth. It can refer to a serious crime that is punishable by death. It can also describe a city that is a center of government; for example, Tallahassee is the capital of Florida. And, it can refer to an uppercase letter, as in *A, B,* or *C. Capital* has a lot of meanings, so remember that the *a* in *capital* stands for *a lot.*

> The word ***capitol*** has only one meaning. It is a building in which the legislature meets. Remember that the *o* in *capitol* stands for *one* and you'll be sure to keep the homophones straight. (For more information about homophones, see page 30.)

> Try drawing a picture that represents as many definitions of *capital* as possible. You might include a lightbulb to show a *capital* idea. Or you could include a map to represent a *capital* city. Be creative! This could help you remember the many times *capital* is spelled with the letter *a.*

Spelling *Accommodate*

▶ Our garage can **accommodate** two **c**ars and two **m**otorcycles.

Accommodate is a word that is often misspelled. It is sometimes spelled with only one *c* or only one *m*. The sentence above can help you remember the correct spelling. "Two **c**ars" can remind you that accommodate has two *c*'s. "Two **m**otorcycles" can help you remember the two *m*'s.

Use colored pencils to write the word *accommodate*. Use a different color for each different letter. For example, use red for the *a*'s, blue for the *c*'s, green for the *o*'s, and so on. You will notice that *accommodate* has two *a*'s and two *o*'s in addition to two *c*'s and two *m*'s. Seeing the patterns in the word can be helpful as you visualize how to spell it correctly in the future.

Than vs. Then

▶ Choose the word **then**
if you're discussing **when**.

The words *then* and *than* are often confused, both in writing and in speech. This rhyme can help you decide which word you need to use.

Then means "at that time." Notice that *then* and *when* have similar spellings. This can help you remember that *then* tells *when*.

Example:

"In school today, we learned about the Jurassic period, Mom. Were you just a baby *then*?"

Than is a conjunction that is used to compare two or more things. Remember that *than* is spelled with an *a*.

Example:

I've read that the average woman lives about five years longer *than* the average man.

One reason many people confuse *than* and *then* is that they do not pronounce the words clearly or correctly. This makes it easy to use the wrong word. Read the example sentences aloud. Be careful to pronounce the vowel sounds in *than* and *then* correctly. *Than* rhymes with *man*. *Then* rhymes with *when*. Being able to hear the differences in the words should help you become aware of which word to use in the future.

Spelling *Occasion*

To correctly spell **occasion,** you must use two *c*'s and one *s.* The two *c*'s that begin the words *Come Celebrate* on the invitation and the *s* in *Special* can help you remember how to spell *occasion.*

Cheerleaders spell out words in a lot of their cheers. Make up a chant or cheer using the letters in *occasion.* You can even use your body to make the shapes of the letters. Then, perform your cheer for a kind friend who promises not to mock you!

. . . .
It's Your Turn

What does your family do for a special *occasion*? Do you *call* your *cousins* and go *swimming*? Do you *color cartoons* and *sing*? Think of a way to make the mnemonic personal so you can remember the two *c*'s and the single *s* in *occasion*.

Principal vs. Principle

▶ The princi**pal** is your **pal**.

Have you ever been unsure of whether to use the word *principal* or *principle*? You're not the only one. This mnemonic is a simple way to remember the difference between the two words.

A **principal** is the head of a school. *Principal* can also mean "most important" or "chief." That makes sense because the *principal* is the "chief" of the school. Just remember that the princi*pal* is your pal (okay, maybe not really, but just play along). The end of the word can help you remember which spelling is correct.

A **principle** is a truth, belief, law, or rule of conduct. To say you are a "person of *principle*" would be a compliment. That means that you stick to your values.

Each of these words has other meanings too. Many scientific laws are called *principles,* such as the principle of conservation of mass. And in banking, *principal* refers to an initial investment.

· · · · · · · · · · · · ·
IT'S YOUR TURN

Look through the newspaper for the words *principal* and *principle*. Highlight these words as you encounter them. Then, underline the words in the surrounding context that help you understand the meaning of the highlighted word.

Stationery vs. Stationary

▶ Stationery   Stationary
         n   n
         v   c
         e   h
         l   o
         o   r
         p   e
         e   d

Stationery and *stationary* are commonly confused words.

Stationery is paper used for writing. If you wanted to write a letter to a friend, you would use stationery. An envelope is an important piece of stationery. The letter **e** for **e**nvelope can help you remember that you will use station**e**ry to send your letter.

Stationary means "fixed" or "unmoving." When a car sits at a red light, it is stationary. That means the car is at a standstill. If something is anchored, that means it is weighted down so that it stays in once place. The letter **a** for **a**nchored can help you remember that something station**a**ry is unmoving.

Imagine a stationary bike at the gym. No matter how fast you pedal, it does not move from its place. In fact, it probably does not even have two wheels. The letter *a* that has replaced the front wheel of this bike can help you remember that something that does not move is *stationary*.

Their, There, and They're

▶ **Their** new house is over **there**, and **they're** moving in today.

Their, there, and *they're* are homophones. They sound the same, but have different meanings and spellings. The mnemonic above uses the words in alphabetical order. This will help you remember the meanings of each.

The first in alphabetical order is *their*. ***Their*** is the possessive form of *they*. In the sentence above, the house belongs to them. It is *their* house.

The next in alphabetical order is *there*. ***There*** means "at that place." In the mnemonic sentence, *there* tells the location of the house.

The last in alphabetical order is *they're*. ***They're*** is a contraction for *they are*. In the mnemonic sentence, *they're* (they are) moving in.

Many people confuse not only when to use *their, there,* and *they're,* but also how to spell each. Look at the word *their. Their* sounds like \a\, so it is an exception to the "i before e" spelling rule.

Look at the word *there*. Notice that it includes the word *here*. This can help you remember that *there* refers to location.

Look at the word *they're*. Remember what you know about contractions. The apostrophe takes the place of the missing letters. This can help you remember that *they're* is short for *they are*.

Boar vs. Bore

▶ B**oar** with an **oar**.
B**ore** for **ore**.

To avoid confusing the spellings of the homonyms *boar* and *bore,* imagine a ***boar*** paddling a canoe with an ***oar.*** This will remind you that the name for a male swine is spelled *boar.* Because miners dig for ore, you can remember that *bore* (which means "to dig deep") contains the word *ore.*

We gave you a picture of a boar rowing a boat with an oar. Now, you should create your own picture of a miner boring for ore to remind yourself of the second part of the mnemonic.

Accept vs. Except

▶ I will **accept** anything, **except** **ex**cuses.

Accept and *except* are homonyms. They sound the same, but are spelled differently. And they have different meanings.

Accept means "to receive" or "to agree to something." You can accept a gift, or you can accept someone's offer to drive you to school.

Except means "but" or "not including." You might like all vegetables except spinach, or you might like every day of the week except Monday.

In the mnemonic sentence, *accept* and *anything* both begin with the letter *a*. *Except* and *excuses* both begin with the letters *ex*.

Picture several objects that belong together, and one object that does not belong. Use a big X to cross off the one that does not belong. All of the items belong except the one with the X. This should help you remember that *except* is spelled with the letter *x*.

Dessert vs. Desert

▶ De**ss**ert has two *s*'s, because it involves **s**omething **s**weet. De**s**ert has one *s*, because it involves **s**and.

The spellings of *dessert* and *desert* are often confused. The only difference is the extra *s* in *dessert*.

You can remember that **dessert** has two *s*'s because dessert is **s**omething **s**weet, like **s**trawberry **s**hortcake.

Desert has only one *s*, because a desert has **s**and. You could also remember that the **S**ahara is a famous desert.

IT'S YOUR TURN

Maybe you're not a big fan of strawberry short-cake. What desserts do you like? See if you can think of something sweet with the initials S. S. that would remind you that *dessert* has two *s*'s.

Words Ending in –ceed

Succeed.
S-U-C-C-E-E-D.
succeed.

▶ Let's give a round of applause for stupendous speller **C. E. Ed**wards. His spelling abilities **exceed** all others'. He will **succeed** in any spelling bee, and he will always **proceed** to the next round!

Only three words in the English language end in –*ceed*. They are *exceed, succeed,* and *proceed.* The sentence above can help you remember them. **C. E. Ed**wards's name can remind you of the –*ceed* pattern. And the three italic words in the story are the only words that end in –*ceed*.

Supersede is the only word in the English language ending in –*sede*.

All other words with the "seed" sound at the end are spelled –*cede*. This is the most common spelling. Examples of words with this spelling include *precede, recede,* and *secede.*

Affect vs. Effect

▶ **Affect shows action.**

Affect and *effect* are commonly confused words. **Affect** is a verb. We know that verbs are action words. *Affect* and *action* both begin with *a*. So, *action* can help you remember that *affect shows action.*

Examples:

How did the unseasonably warm weather *affect* your ski vacation?

All of the Cs on my report card will *affect* my curfew this weekend—and not in a positive way.

Effect is a noun or a thing. An *effect* is the result or consequence of an action. Think of the phrase *cause and effect* to remember that an effect is an outcome.

Examples:

We learned about the *effects* of fuel emissions on the environment.

What was the *effect* of your sister's decision to go to college halfway across the country?

When using the words *affect* and *effect,* be careful to pronounce them clearly. The beginning of *affect* sounds like *affair* or *affirmative*. The beginning of *effect* sounds like *effort* or *efficient*. Emphasize the beginning sound, and soon you will learn to hear the difference between the two words.

Author's Purpose

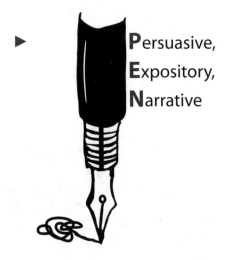

▶ **P**ersuasive,
Expository,
Narrative

Knowing why an author wrote a particular piece can be helpful in understanding what you read. To find the **author's purpose,** ask yourself *why* he or she wrote the text. There are three basic types of texts. Each serves a different purpose.

Persuasive text is written to convince the reader of something. An editorial about the need for more gym class in schools would be persuasive text.

Expository text is written to inform or teach the reader. An essay about life in a small village in Tanzania would be an expository piece.

Narrative text is written to entertain the reader. A fictional story about an eighty-year-old trapeze artist who wins the lottery would be considered a narrative.

The acronym PEN is made of the first letter of each of the types of text. Remembering this mnemonic can help you determine the author's purpose when you read. And, because an author may use a *pen* when he or she writes, this one should be easy to remember.

 *Get This . . .*

Did you know that with the increasing popularity of e-mail and instant messaging, acronyms have become more popular too? You may be using acronyms every day without even realizing it! Some of the popular Internet acronyms include:

LOL (laughing out loud)
DQMOT (Don't quote me on this.)
BRB (Be right back.)
IM (instant message)
TTFN (Ta-ta for now.)

Other acronyms you may hear every day include NASA, LASER, and LCD. See if you can find out what each stands for. Then, pay attention to how many other acronyms you come across today. **99**

Genre

▶ **Never play piano beside short referees.**

A **genre** is a type of literary work. Just as there are lots of different types of movies (horror, comedy, documentary, and so on), there are many types of literary works. The first letter in each word of the acrostic stands for one of the literary genres below.

- **novel**
- **play**
- **poem**
- **biography**
- **short story**
- **reference book**

Some of the words in the mnemonic also sound like the genres they represent. For example, the word *play* in the acrostic stands for the genre play, the word *short* stands for short stories, and the word *referees* stands for reference book. Keeping this image and the acrostic in mind should help you remember these genres.

In order for an acrostic to help you remember a set of information, you first have to remember the acrostic itself! One way to reinforce this acrostic is by pantomiming the act of playing piano beside short referees. To pantomime means "to express a story by moving your body."

Find a bench or a chair that you can pretend is a piano bench. Act out squeezing onto the bench between two other people. Then, pretend you are playing the piano with your arms squeezed to your sides. To get across the idea that you are beside *short* referees, you may look down at them irritably. Or, you could pretend to switch places with one of the referees. Then, you could hunch down to appear short and pretend to blow a whistle or gesture like you're calling a time-out. It may sound silly, but you'll never forget the sentence!

Narrative Elements

▶ **Certain Sporty Cows Play Racquetball.**

Narrative elements are the parts of a story that work together to make the narrative interesting, vivid, and meaningful. The first letter in each word of the acrostic stands for one of the narrative elements below.

- **Characters:** the people, animals, or even imaginary beings in a story
- **Setting:** where and when a story takes place
- **Conflict:** the main problem that the characters in a story face
- **Plot:** the series of events that happen in a story
- **Resolution:** how the conflict gets resolved at the end of a story

. . . .
IT'S YOUR TURN

Keep a detailed journal for a week. Then, put the journal away somewhere so you won't be tempted to read it. After another week passes, try to recall the most interesting thing that happened to you during the journal week. See if you can recall any details about the event and the order in which things happened. Then, compare your memory against your journal account. How accurate was your memory of what happened?

Stanzas

▶ "Stands apart"

Many poems are divided into separate sections, based on a certain number of lines or a certain rhyme pattern. Each of these sections of several lines in a poem is called a **stanza.** Stanzas are sometimes referred to as *verses.*

The keywords "stands apart" can help you remember that the separate sections of a poem are called *stanzas.* Each stanza in a poem stands apart—they are usually separated by line spaces.

 Look at the following poem by William Blake. The poem has two stanzas. Notice how the stanzas stand apart.

The Sick Rose

O Rose, thou art sick!
The invisible worm
That flies in the night,
In the howling storm,

Has found out thy bed
Of crimson joy:
And his dark secret love
Does thy life destroy.

The Sonnet

A **sonnet** is a 14-line poem. There are two types of sonnets. Each follows a specific rhyme pattern.

The first type of sonnet is the *Shakespearean* sonnet. These poems have 3 stanzas of 4 lines each, followed by a 2-line stanza. The 4-line stanzas are called *quatrains*. The 2-line stanza is a *couplet*. The rhyme pattern is usually *abab cdcd efef gg*.

The second type of sonnet is the *Italian* sonnet. These have an 8-line stanza followed by a 6-line stanza. The 8-line stanza is called an *octave*. The 6-line stanza is called a *sestet*. The rhyme pattern of the octave is usually *abbaabba*. The rhyme pattern of the sestet is usually *cdecde*.

The acronym SIR F. P. SONNET, the name of the fictional poet in the illustration on the next page, can help you remember the definition of a sonnet. SIR F. P. stands for **Shakespearean** or **Italian, rhyming, fourteen-line poems.** And of course, the last name helps you remember that this mnemonic defines a sonnet.

The picture of this fictional poet can help you remember the facts about sonnets. Sir F. P. Sonnet looks like he could be a character in a Shakespearean play, which will help you remember the Shakespearean sonnet. His left boot is shaped like the country of Italy, which stands for the Italian sonnet. And finally, on the desk beside him is a sheet with some writing, which reminds you that a sonnet is a poem. The paper shows the number 14, which will help you remember that a sonnet has 14 lines.

Limericks

▶ **Limericks** are fun five-line poems.
They're easy to write once you know 'em.
Lines 1, 2, and 5,
and lines 3 and 4 rhyme.
With this rhythm, your poem is golden!

A **limerick** is a five-line poem with an *aabba* rhyme pattern. The first, second, and fifth lines have seven to ten syllables, and these lines all rhyme. The third and fourth lines have five to seven syllables and rhyme with each other. Named after an Irish town called Limerick, these poems are often silly or nonsensical.

The poem at the top of the page is an example of a limerick. It is also a mnemonic device that will remind you of the characteristics of a limerick.

Read the nursery rhyme "Hickory Dickory Dock" below. Listen to the rhythm. Notice how the first, second, and fifth lines rhyme. Notice that lines three and four rhyme also.

Hickory Dickory Dock.
The mouse ran up the clock.
The clock struck one,
the mouse ran down.
Hickory Dickory Dock.

- - - - - - - - - - - -
IT'S YOUR TURN

Try to write your own limerick. It can be about anything. Use the example at the top of the page to remind you of what you will need to include in your poem. And be as silly as possible!

Structure of a Paragraph

▶ Three students sat stacking cheeseburgers.

A well-written paragraph should include three things: a topic sentence, three supporting details, and a concluding sentence. The first letter in each word of this acrostic stands for one part of a paragraph. *Three* represents the topic sentence. *Students, sat,* and *stacking* each stand for a supporting detail. *Cheeseburgers* represents the concluding sentence.

The **topic sentence** introduces the main idea of the paragraph. Its purpose is to summarize what the paragraph is about and catch the reader's interest. It is the most general sentence and does not include many details.

The next sentences make up the body of the paragraph. They include at least **three supporting details,** facts, or examples. Their purpose is to explain what was introduced in the topic sentence.

The **concluding sentence** is last. It restates the main idea, using different words from the topic sentence.

Use the image of this cheeseburger to help you remember the structure of a paragraph. The topic sentence is the top bun. The supporting details are the cheese, the burger, and the lettuce. The concluding sentence is the bottom bun. In a lot of ways, a paragraph is like a cheeseburger. The top and bottom are similar—holding everything together—while all the good stuff is in the middle. But, if you add too many extras, you end up with a real mess!

Writing an Essay

Step one in writing an essay is to **research.** Your resources could include reference books, articles, interviews, or information found online.

▶ Remember, *one* rhymes with *bun.* Think of the picture of the reference book on a bun.

Step two is to **plan and outline** your paper. An outline is the "bare bones" of your paper. You will add details and supporting information to fatten up your essay later.

The skeleton in the shoe can help you remember this step. *Two* rhymes with *shoe.*

Step three is to *write* your essay.

Three rhymes with *tree*. Think of the pencil tree to remember this step.

Step four is to *revise* your work. Edit the language, add or delete information, and rearrange text so that it is organized and effective.

See the corrected text all over the door. *Door* rhymes with *four*.

> **" Get This . . .**
>
> Pegword mnemonics can be used to remember all kinds of things. These picture clues have even proven helpful in memorizing phone numbers. To do this, think of the picture associated with each digit. Then, create a story that involves these pictures in the correct order. Pegwords have also been helpful for many students when learning math facts. For example, to remember that $3 \times 4 = 12$, you can picture a tree (three) with a hidden door (four) in its trunk. An elf (the pegword for 12) is opening the door. **"**

Step five is to prepare your *final copy*.

Remember a picture of a beehive coming out of a printer. *Five* rhymes with *hive*.

Foreshadowing

► **FOUR SHADOWING**

Foreshadowing is a literary technique through which hints are given to suggest what will happen later in a story. In this illustration, the four monsters' giant shadows *foreshadow* trouble for the character.

One famous example of foreshadowing occurs at the beginning of the movie *The Wizard of Oz*. During the early scenes in Kansas, Dorothy talks with three farmhands and a mean old lady named Miss Gulch. Each of these characters sets up a later role. The farmhands reappear in Oz as the Scarecrow, the Tin Man, and the Cowardly Lion; the mean old lady reappears in Oz as the Wicked Witch of the West.

In one example of foreshadowing, the farmhand who later appears as the Cowardly Lion advises Dorothy to be brave. The audience soon discovers, however, that this farmhand is frightened of hogs. This scene foreshadows the Cowardly Lion's gutless behavior in Oz.

In another example, Miss Gulch wants to have the dog Toto "destroyed" and Dorothy calls her a "wicked old witch." This clearly foreshadows the arrival of the Wicked Witch of the West in Oz.

Turn out all of the lights except for one lamp and use your hands as shadow puppets to act out a dramatic scene. You could hold your left hand so that it resembles a stick figure and wiggle the four fingers on your right hand as if they were slithering snakes creeping toward the figure. The four shadows of the "snakes" foreshadow that something bad is going to happen to that poor stick figure! This will reinforce the keywords "four shadowing."

Stream of Consciousness

Once I met this guy who had these lamb chop sideburns. He had an accent and may have been from Yugoslavia. That's a country that doesn't exist anymore. Anyway, this guy was wearing the strangest hat. I had never seen a hat like he was wearing and I could not take my eyes off of his hat, and he asked...

Stream of consciousness is a literary technique. Writers use stream of consciousness to represent the scattershot way in which the human mind works. Stream of consciousness writing often includes partial sentences, nonsense sentences, half-formed thoughts and ideas, and long passages lacking logic or focus.

Famous works of literature that use stream of consciousness narrative include William Faulkner's *As I Lay Dying,* James Joyce's *Ulysses,* Henry Roth's *Call It Sleep,* and Virginia Woolf's *To the Lighthouse.* T. S. Eliot's famous poem "The Love Song of J. Alfred Prufrock" also employs stream of consciousness.

It's Your Turn

Write one page of your own stream of consciousness. You might start by writing about a stream, and then see where your mind goes from there. Hopefully, you'll find that it's fun to go on a tangent!

Simile

▶ "Smiley"

A **simile** makes a comparison between two unlike things, using either the word *like* or the word *as*. Similes focus on what is similar between the two things. So, when your aunt says, "Oh, you are growing like a weed," she is not saying you are actually a weed. She is using a simile to compare how fast you are growing to how fast a weed grows.

The mnemonic uses the word *like* twice. The *like* in "I *like* chocolate" means the girl enjoys chocolate. The *like* in "it's just like heaven" is part of a simile comparing chocolate to heaven. You may be "smiley" if you like something, which will help you remember that a simile says something is *like* something else. When you hear the word *simile*, think of the keyword "smiley" and recall the silly picture above.

Draw a picture that shows a literal interpretation of a simile. For example, maybe you hear the same annoying pop song on the radio every day and you can't get the tune out of your head. You could say, "That song is like bubble gum that sticks to my brain." Of course you wouldn't mean it literally. But if you did, what would it look like?

Metaphor

"The *metal fork* thought life was a piece of cake."

A **metaphor** makes a comparison between two unlike things, but does not use the words *like* or *as*. Usually, metaphors use *to be* verbs, saying that one thing *is* or *was* another thing in order to create a vivid image or make a dramatic point.

Examples:

Your *friend's bad attitude is a lead weight*—you should be enjoying summer vacation, not sulking in her bedroom.

My *attic bedroom was a furnace* until I "borrowed" the fan from my little brother's room while he was at basketball practice.

The mnemonic at the top of the page will help you remember the definition of *metaphor*. The keywords "metal fork" sound like *metaphor,* which will remind you that the sentence is a clue about metaphor. The joke comparing the fork's life to a piece of cake will help you remember that a metaphor compares two unlike things. In this cartoon, the fork's life is a piece of cake both literally (his days revolve around digging into desserts) and metaphorically (his life is pretty easy).

. . . .
IT'S YOUR TURN

Think of ways to complete these metaphors.

Her screeching voice was
_____.

The tiny bedroom was
_____.

The sound of their laughter was _____.

Remember, don't use the words *like* or *as* in your metaphors—then they'd be similes.

Onomatopoeia

Onomatopoeia is the use of words that imitate sounds, like *buzz* and *bang*. The words on the cereal box—*pop, crackle, crunch, munch,* and *splash*—are examples of words that sound like the noises they describe.

Think of examples of onomatopoeia. Say the words aloud dramatically, making them sound the way the actual sounds do. Mimic the sharp "crack" of a baseball bat. Imitate the menacing "hiss" of a slithering snake. See if you can recreate the "pop" of a balloon bursting.

Alliteration

▶ Seven spotted swans sat speaking in the sun,
using words with first letter repetition.
"What are these similar starting sounds?" asked one.
"My feathered friend, it's alliteration."

Alliteration is the repetition of a beginning consonant sound. This technique is most commonly used in poetry. Writers use alliteration to emphasize phrases or to make the writing sound more musical, or rhythmic.

In the rhyme above, there are three examples of alliteration. The first line repeats the beginning \s\ sound. The third line also repeats the \s\ sound. The last line repeats the beginning \f\ sound.

Learning the poem above will help you remember the meaning of alliteration.

Think of some tongue twisters you know that use alliteration, such as "Peter Piper" or "She Sells Sea Shells." Try reciting them aloud. Notice the emphasis on the first consonant sound and listen to the repetition of that sound. Alliteration is a way to make writing interesting, but it can also confuse your tongue!

" *Get This* ...

Using rhymes, rhythm, and melody is a common way to memorize. In fact, you have probably been doing this for years. The first things you ever memorized were probably nursery rhymes.

People have been using rhymes to help them recall information for centuries. Many ancient Greek stories, such as Homer's *Odyssey*, were told in the form of epic poems repeated from memory. The storytellers used rhythm, rhyme, and repetition to remember the stories. And if you've ever read Homer, you know these stories aren't short! **"**

Coordinating Conjunctions

► **F**or
And
Nor
But
Or
Yet
So

Coordinating conjunctions are words used to join the two parts of a compound sentence. The conjunctions are *for, and, nor, but, or, yet,* and *so.*

Examples:

We wanted to buy the new video game, *but* my dad thought it was too violent.

I didn't want to open the letter, *for* I was afraid the news would be bad.

My New Year's resolution is to eat better, *so* I'm giving up chocolate donuts.

You can use the acronym FANBOYS to remember the coordinating conjunctions. Each letter in the acronym is the first letter of one of the conjunctions.

And in case you're wondering, a fanboy is a guy who is totally obsessed with a certain hobby or an object of entertainment—usually TV shows, movies (a particular sci-fi trilogy comes to mind), comic books, or video games. A fanboy takes his subject very seriously and knows all the details about it. It may help you remember this acronym to picture a guy who is obsessed with grammar, wearing a "Conjunctions are cool!" T-shirt.

❝Get This . . .

In the 1970s, a series of short, educational cartoons were produced by Schoolhouse Rock. These were aired between Saturday morning cartoons. They were originally created by the owner of an advertising agency as a way to help his son with his schoolwork.

In 1973, the song "Conjunction Junction" aired for the first time. The lyrics were supposed to help kids remember the "uses" of a conjunction. The lyrics rhymed, and the cartoon had silly images and characters, which helped kids remember the information.

You can visit the Web site, www.school-house-rock.com to see the lyrics or listen to the song. ❞

Run-on Sentences

▶ "Run-into" sentences

A **run-on sentence** is two complete sentences or unrelated statements incorrectly joined together without proper punctuation between them.

Example:

While visiting the zoo, we ate popcorn a kangaroo and the spider monkeys were my favorite animals.

In other words, the two sentences "run into" each other. This can completely change the meaning of what you have written. You wouldn't want someone to think you had eaten popcorn, a kangaroo, and the spider monkeys, would you? To avoid these wrecks of wordage, think of punctuation as the stop sign that will keep the two sentences apart.

Example:

While visiting the zoo, we ate popcorn. A kangaroo and the spider monkeys were my favorite animals.

👁 To help remember this clue, picture the two sentences in a run-on actually having a head-on collision. Then, picture a stop sign placed between the end of one sentence and the beginning of the next.

SCREEEEECH!!

Prefixes, Base Words, and Suffixes

▶ **P**refix
Baseword
Suffix

The familiar acronym PBS usually refers to a public television network. But it can also remind you of the order of these word parts: prefix, base word, suffix.

A **prefix** is added to the beginning of a base word to modify the meaning. Common prefixes are *re–, un–, dis–, non–,* and *extra–*. Adding *un–* to the beginning of the word means "not," as in *unhappy*.

The **base word** is the part of a word that has meaning. It is sometimes called the *root word*. In the word *unbelievable, believe* is the base word.

A **suffix** is added to the end of the base word to alter the meaning or the part of speech. Common suffixes include *–ing, –ly, –ness, –able,* and *–ful*. Adding *–able* to the end of a verb makes it an adjective, as in *likeable*.

Look at the word *unthinkable. Un–* is the prefix, *think* is the base word, and *–able* is the suffix.

un + think + able = unthinkable

Write the words below on index cards. Use scissors to cut apart the prefixes, base words, and suffixes. (Some words do not have both a prefix and a suffix.) Separate the word parts by moving them to different parts of a table. Place prefixes on the far left, base words in the middle, and suffixes on the far right. Then, try mixing up the word parts to make new words.

unlikely, unhappiness, removable, disturbing, rereading, careful, quietly, unstoppable, playful, mistake, befriended, bicyclist, antisocial, ownership, cooperate

Prepositions

▶ "What position?"

A **preposition** is a part of speech. It is usually used before a noun in a phrase that modifies another part of the sentence. For example, in the sentence "I left my basketball in the driveway," the preposition is *in* and the prepositional phrase is *in the driveway*.

Notice that the prepositional phrase tells us *where* the basketball was left. Prepositions are often used to describe position.

Examples:

under the sycamore tree	*over* their heads
toward the back door	*around* her wrist
into outer space	*beneath* the bed

Whenever you ask the position of an object, chances are that the answer will begin with a preposition. That's why the keywords "What position?" can help you remember the meaning of *preposition*.

Look at the following sentence:

There was a bike path around the lake.

Ask yourself which word in the sentence tells us about position. *Around* is the preposition, and *around the lake* is the prepositional phrase.

Keep in mind that not all prepositions describe position. For example, you might say "Terrell was the winner *of* the spelling bee" or "The movie was *about* bank robbers." The words *of* and *about* are both prepositions, but they don't tell *where*. Sometimes prepositions answer the question "Which one?" or "What kind?"

Linking Verbs

There are several different types of verbs, including action verbs, helping verbs, and linking verbs. Action verbs show action, as in "She *walks* to school." Helping verbs usually come before the main (action) verb of a sentence and often show tense: "Marco *will* bring the brownies." **Linking verbs** describe a state of being, and they usually connect an adjective to a noun.

Examples:

Marisa *seems* older when she wears her glasses.
The lake *looks* peaceful in the wintertime.
If you leave milk in the refrigerator for too long, it *turns* sour.
Those chocolate chip cookies *smell* terrific!
If you don't *remain* silent, they'll find your hiding space!

Keep in mind that some verbs can be used as *either* action verbs or linking verbs. For example, in the sample sentence above, *looks* is used as a linking verb because it is describing the condition of the lake. But in the sentence "Jane looks out the window at the lake," the word *looks* is being used as an action verb. Do you see the difference?

The following are thirteen of the most common linking verbs. (Of course, other forms of these verbs are linking verbs too.)

appear, be, become, look, feel, grow, seem, smell, sound, taste, remain, turn, stay

▶ In order to remember these 13 linking verbs, chunk them into categories.

5 verbs that describe a current condition:	3 verbs that describe a change of condition:	5 verbs that describe conditions noticed by the senses:
• seem	• become	• look
• be	• grow	• sound
• appear	• turn	• smell
• remain		• taste
• stay		• feel

Lay versus Lie

▶ **Lay** the filet on the silver tray,
Lie in the sty 'neath the starry sky.

Have you ever been corrected for saying that you were so tired, you just wanted to go "lay down" in bed? You wouldn't be the first person to confuse the verbs *lay* and *lie*.

The verb **lay** means "to set something down." You've probably heard of a bricklayer. A bricklayer is not someone who likes to sleep on a pile of bricks, of course! A bricklayer is a craftsman who sets bricks during a construction project.

Example:

"Time is up. Please close your test booklets and *lay* your pencils down on the table."

The verb **lie** means "to rest, or recline in a horizontal position." You can remember that *lay* is the more active verb ("lay the book on the table"), while *lie* is a passive verb ("the books are lying on the table").

Example:

I almost look forward to catching a cold, so I have an excuse to *lie* on the couch all day and read magazines!

Use the rhyming mnemonic above to help keep these verbs straight. Next time you're feeling exhausted, imagine a cook laying a filet on a tray and a pig lying in a sty under the sky, and then go *lie down!*

❝ *Get This . . .*

To make matters even more confusing, *lay* and *lie* are both irregular verbs. (For more information about irregular verbs, see page 42.) The past tense of *lay* is *laid,* and the past tense of *lie* is actually *lay!* Because English has more irregularities in its spelling system than many other alphabetic languages, it is a difficult language to read and write. Instead of learning rules and sounding out words phonetically, a learner of English has to memorize a lot of special cases. Studies have even shown that English speakers have a higher rate of dyslexia than speakers of other languages. Mnemonics can be useful in helping English-learners memorize rules, but the best way to master all of the quirks is to be an avid reader! ❞

Using Capital Letters

▶ When visiting politicians in a nation's **capital**, it is **proper first** to **greet** everyone, then to **quote** your name and **title**, and finally to **close** the door as you leave.

You can use this mnemonic to remember the rules for using **capital letters.** Capitalize the following:

- **proper** nouns (April, Friday, Thanksgiving, Henry)
- the **first word** in a sentence
- the first word in the **greeting** of a letter (Dear Prudence, To whom it may concern)
- the first word in a **quote**
- a **title** preceding a name (Dr., Miss, Colonel)
- the first word in the **closing** of a letter (Yours truly, Best wishes)

Write the mnemonic on a sheet of paper. Underline each keyword, or write them in a different color. Then, read the sentence several times. Turn the paper over and see if you can write the mnemonic from memory. Write the capitalization rule that each keyword represents.

Write a short letter that applies each of the capitalization rules. It needs to be only one or two sentences long. You can even use the following format:

[Greeting] [Title] [Proper Noun],

[First word], I saw a [strange animal] at the zoo, and it [weird thing an animal might do]. That's when I said, "[Quote]." That's a funny story, huh?

[Closing],

[Your name]

Look at the letter for a few minutes, then try writing it from memory. See if you remember all the rules.

Using Commas

▶ I came into the house, and yelled "hello" to **greet** my mother. I **closed** the front door and went into the kitchen to see her. She was writing the grocery **list**. "What's going on this afternoon?" I asked. She told me to check the **date** on the calendar. I walked to the calendar and realized we had a lot of **places** to hit, and the grocery store was just the beginning. I was **sentenced** to a day full of boring errands.

There are several rules for using **commas.** The highlighted words in the paragraph stand for these rules. As you read the mnemonic, picture yourself following the same steps listed in the story. This will help you remember the keywords for the comma rules.

- A comma follows the **greeting** of a letter. (Dear Aunt Mary,)
- A comma follows the **closing** of a letter. (Your son, John)
- A comma is used to separate items in a **list.** (We need to buy milk, eggs, and bread.)
- A comma is used between the day and the year in a **date.** (July 4, 1776)
- A comma is used between the names of **places,** such as a city and state, or a city and country. (Tampa, Florida; London, England)
- A comma is used before the conjunction in a **compound sentence.** (We were going to bake a cake, but there wasn't any flour in the house.)

Begin at your front door, and walk through your house acting out this mnemonic as you read it. Greet your mom, close the door, walk to the kitchen, and check the calendar. Do this several times to help you remember the clue words.

Uses of a Period

▶ **"I am just a SAD period☹"**

The acronym SAD represents the three main uses of a **period.**

- Use a period at the end of a **sentence.** Remember, periods follow sentences that tell.

- Use a period following an **abbreviation.** (Dr., Oct., or Mrs.)

- Use a period as a **decimal point.** (99.9% or $57.25)

As you read this page, stomp your foot every time you come to a period that ends a sentence. Then, pick up any book or magazine, and do the same thing. This will emphasize the primary function of periods, which is creating pauses, or breaks, in a text.

❝ *Get This . . .*

SAD is an acronym. An *acronym* is an abbreviation formed from the first letters in a list of words. It actually comes from the Greek words *akros* meaning "beginning" and *nym* meaning "name" or "word." But have you ever wondered if the word *acronym* could be an acronym itself?

A Clever **R**eminder **O**f **N**ames **Y**ou **M**istake

Anyone **C**an **R**ecall **O**bscure **N**uggets—**Y**ea **M**nemonics!

Abbreviated **C**odes **R**etain **O**dd **N**ames in **Y**our **M**emory ❞

Apostrophes

ap**OP**strophes

The letters in the word POP stand for the first letter in each of the three uses of **apostrophes.** Apostrophes are used to indicate:

- **Possessive nouns** (*Sandra's face, women's rights, the dogs' collars*)

- **Omitted letters or numbers** (*don't, I'll, rock 'n' roll, tug o' war, the '80s*)

- **Plurals of lowercase letters or words in quotation marks** (*three m's, four q's, many "thank-you's", several "not applicable's"*)

Using an apostrophe to show possession can get a little tricky. In order to form the possessive of a singular noun, we add *'s* (*Colorado's capital*). To form the possessive of a plural noun that ends in *s*, we simply add an apostrophe (*the two boys' faces*). To form the possessive of a plural noun that doesn't end in s, add *'s* (*children's books*).

Write a list of phrases containing apostrophes. Be sure to include examples of each rule on this page. Then, use a bright-colored marker to trace over each apostrophe. Look at each word. The colored apostrophe should stand out. Notice placement of the apostrophe in each example and think about which rule is represented.

Remember the Alamo,
**   and everything else...**

Early Settlements in the New World

The English settled in several places in the New World in the late 1500s and 1600s. The first English settlement was in 1585 at **Roanoke,** Virginia. Next was **Jamestown** in 1607. The Pilgrims arrived at **Plymouth Rock** in 1620. Then, the Puritans founded the **Massachusetts Bay Colony** in 1630. Finally, **Pennsylvania** was founded as an English colony in 1681.

To help you remember the order of these settlements, look at the drawings connected to each pegword.

▶ *One* rhymes with *bun*. See a bun rowing a boat with the word "Row-anoke" carved into it and think of Roanoke.

Two rhymes with *shoe*. See James living in a shoe and think of Jamestown.

❝ *Get This . . .*

An interesting fact about these early colonies is that the colony at Roanoke mysteriously vanished. The colony was short on food and other supplies, and the founder, John White, sailed back to England to get supplies. He was unable to return for three years, and when he did, he found that all one hundred colonists were gone. The only clue was a mysterious word, *Croatoan*, carved into a tree. No one ever discovered what had happened to the colonists. **❞**

Three rhymes with *tree*. See the tree growing out of a big rock and think of Plymouth Rock.

Plymouth Rock

Four rhymes with *door*. See the door floating on a bay and think of the Massachusetts Bay Colony.

Massachusetts Bay

Five rhymes with *hive*. See the bees writing on their hive with big fat pens and think of Pennsylvania.

Close your eyes and try to visualize each image in order. If you forget one picture in the series, open your eyes, "photograph" that image in your mind, and try again.

The Navigation Acts of 1651

I walk into the antique store, and *to my right is a shelf* with models of **English ships**. The tag says they are toys from the mid-1600s. I ask my mom if I can play with one, but she has wandered to *the back of the store*. There, I find her looking at some old-fashioned wood containers labeled **tobacco**, **sugar**, and other things. "These would look great in our kitchen," she says. Decorating is boring, so I drift over to look at some textiles hanging on the *left wall* of the store. The colorful cloths must have been **imports** from Asia. On the way out, *at the cash register,* my mother complains about how high the sales **tax** is. And we leave the store with her containers, but without my ships.

The **Navigation Acts** were a series of laws passed by England about overseas trade and the English colonies. The highlighted words in this story stand for four provisions of the Navigation Acts. Each rule was designed to make sure that England profited from any colonial trading and that it had access to colonial resources.

The italicized words are the locations in the store that can help you remember each rule. Using the loci technique, you can imagine yourself standing in the store, looking around at each item in its place; the items should remind you of the four laws.

The following are four provisions of the Navigation Acts of 1651–1663:

1. All goods exported from English colonies must be carried in **English ships.**

2. Certain colonial goods such as **tobacco and sugar** could be sold only to England.

3. **Imports** must be sent to England first before going to the English colonies.

4. A **tax** was charged on all goods made in English colonies that were not sent to England.

❝ Get This . . .

Did someone ever suggest that you retrace your steps to remember where you left something? For example, maybe you remember you had your yo-yo at the supermarket, because you almost flung it into a jar of pickles. Then, you remember waiting in line while your dad paid for the groceries. Next, you walked out of the store—but wait! You also fished around in your pockets to see if you had a quarter for the gumball machine. You pulled out some gum wrappers and threw them in the garbage can, and you put the yo-yo on top of the gumball machine once you found a quarter. It must still be there on top of the gumball machine! This is an example of using the loci method in everyday life. By picturing yourself journeying through a series of locations, you can better remember a specific event. **❞**

The Thirteen Original Colonies

▶ "Noah's mangy cat required nine painful needles!" declared my vet's new secretary, Gus.

This acrostic can help you remember the names of the **thirteen original colonies** that would eventually become the United States. The first letter in each word of the sentence stands for one of these colonies. This acrostic also presents the colonies in geographical order. The colony represented by the first word, **N**ew Hampshire, is the farthest north. The colony represented by the last word, **G**eorgia, is the farthest south.

Below is a list of the thirteen original colonies, from north to south.

1. **New Hampshire**
2. **Massachusetts**
3. **Connecticut**
4. **Rhode Island**
5. **New York**
6. **Pennsylvania**
7. **New Jersey**
8. **Delaware**
9. **Maryland**
10. **Virginia**
11. **North Carolina**
12. **South Carolina**
13. **Georgia**

Once you have memorized the sentence, write down the first letter of each word on a piece of paper. Try to fill in each letter with the colony the letter represents. You may want to refer to a map to help you at first. Be aware that there are four colonies that all start with the letter *N* in this list—make sure to note their geographical order. Keep trying this exercise until you get every colony in the correct order.

If you use a current map of the East Coast of the United States, you will notice some major differences. Maine and Florida were not part of the original colonies. Also, Virginia was eventually split into Virginia and West Virginia.

Revolutionary War Events

The Declaration of Independence was adopted on July 4, 1776, asserting that the American colonies would be independent of British rule. Do you know what happened next? To remember the sequence of the important events in the Revolutionary War, imagine yourself walking through a house. Each room in the house contains one important event.

▶ To remember these events in order, imagine yourself walking through the rooms in the following order. (The words in italics connect each event to its room to make it more memorable.)

Living Room: the **Declaration of Independence** was signed in 1776. The Americans wanted to *live* independent of British rule and stated this officially.

Closet: the **Battles of Saratoga**. Imagine a *toga* hanging in the closet to remember the Battles of Saratoga. These battles were a turning point of the war, as the Americans soundly defeated the British troops.

Kitchen: **France enters the war** on the American side. (Remember: The French are known for being great *cooks*.)

Laundry room: the **Battle of Yorktown**. General George Washington led the American and French troops to the decisive victory of the war. The British were all *washed up*.

Bedroom: The **Treaty of Paris** ends the war in 1783. The British agreed to the let the former colonies become a free and independent country, and the conflict was *put to bed*.

· · · · · · · · · · · · ·
IT'S YOUR TURN

Think of another series of facts or events you want to remember in order—perhaps the first five U.S. presidents. In your notebook, draw a simple diagram or floor plan of your house or apartment. Be sure to include as many rooms in the diagram as there are things you want to remember. You can even include hallways, porches, and closets, if needed. Fill in your diagram by drawing a different president in each room, and then close your eyes and take a mental walk through the house. Did you remember what each room stood for? Did you walk through the locations in the correct order?

The Treaty of Paris of 1783

▶ Having **independent** access to a private pond with clearly defined **boundaries** is a **fishing** enthusiast's dream. Fishermen hate to feel **enslaved** to pay off the traditional **debt** (giving away their best catch) for fishing on another man's **property**.

The American colonists won the Revolutionary War in 1783. After eight long years of fighting, they won the right to send the English soldiers away. Before allowing the English to leave, however, they had them sign the Treaty of Paris of 1783. This treaty put an end to the war by clearly stating that the United States was no longer an English property. There were other key terms that the colonists included in the treaty. The highlighted words in the chaining mnemonic stand for the six major terms of the treaty.

The following are the six major terms agreed upon in the Treaty of Paris of 1783:

1. The United States was now an **independent** nation.

2. The **boundaries** of this new nation were agreed upon.

3. **Fishing** rights were to be granted to the United States in key English locations.

4. **Slaves** taken by the English troops would be returned and all prisoners would be freed.

5. **Debts** that were owed before the war would be paid back by both sides.

6. **Property** taken by the colonies from Loyalists would be returned.

. . . .
IT'S YOUR TURN

Maybe fishing doesn't interest you at all. If this story is difficult for you to remember, try to create your own story using the same keywords. You may put the highlighted words in a different order. Just remember that the sentence you create should be memorable for you.

Manifest Destiny

▶ "Mani-feast" Destiny

Manifest Destiny was the belief in the 1800s that the United States was destined to take over all the land west to the Pacific Ocean. Many people felt they had the right and the duty to spread the nation's ideals across the continent. Unfortunately, this pursuit led to bloody wars against Native Americans and Mexico. The keyword *feast* sounds like –*fest,* and you can eat greedily and take all the food you want in a feast. You can use this keyword mnemonic to remember that people who believed in Manifest Destiny wanted to consume all the land.

👁 A strong visual always helps to reinforce a keyword mnemonic. For example, to remember "Mani-feast" Destiny, you might imagine someone with a very large mouth trying to eat an entire table set for a feast, and the table could be covered with large plates that hold the Oregon Territory, Texas, and other areas in the soon-to-be western and southwestern United States.

The Cherokee under Andrew Jackson's Democracy

▶ Andrew Jackson's new democracy,
did not apply to the Cherokee.
And it only got worse over the years,
with tragedies like the Trail of Tears.

Andrew Jackson, the seventh president of the United States, was very popular for being a man of the people. His "new" democracy valued the public good and put the rights of the common man above the elite. Sadly, however, he did not consider the Cherokee and other Native Americans to be worthy of the same rights.

To expand U.S. territory, Jackson took every opportunity to force Native Americans to move farther west. He forced Native Americans to accept treaties that made it legal for the United States to take their land away. In 1832, the Supreme Court said that state governments could not make laws forcing the Cherokee people to leave. Jackson defied this ruling and organized federal troops to force the **Cherokee** out of Georgia. The Cherokee were marched hundreds of miles west along what is known as the **Trail of Tears.** About 4,000 of them died along the way. Jackson's disregard for the rights and the lives of Native Americans had terrible long-term effects, including war.

❝ *Get This . . .*

Did you know that, just like there are rules of the road, there are also rules for boating? Boaters must know who has the right of way if two boats are approaching each other, so that they don't collide. They also need to understand the system of different colored lights that boats use to communicate at night. For example, if a boat is displaying one red light over another red light, it means that the boat is unattended. This might mean that the captain is sleeping, or it could mean that the boat is anchored. To remember what two red lights mean, captains use the rhyming mnemonic, 'Red over red, this boat is dead,' or 'Red over red, captain's in bed.' **❞**

Effects of the California Gold Rush

▶ SCENE

In 1848, gold was discovered in present-day Sacramento, California, at a place called Sutter's Mill. By the next year, California was flooded with people hoping to strike it rich. "Gold Fever" had major effects on an enormous number of people. Although the journey to California was very dangerous, the possibility of finding gold was too tempting for many to resist. While few miners actually struck it rich, there were many other effects of the Gold Rush. The letters in the acronym SCENE stand for the five major effects of the **California Gold Rush.**

- **Statehood for California:** The population increased so rapidly in 1849 that California was allowed to become a state in 1850.

- *Californios* **lost their land and culture:** The original Mexican inhabitants of California were soon outnumbered and their way of life suffered.

- **Economic growth:** The huge growth in population created new businesses of every type, from farming to shipping and banking.

- **Native Americans were killed:** Two out of every three Native Americans in the area were killed, either by new diseases or racial intolerance.

- **Enslaved people were freed:** Because California was admitted as a free state, the slaves in California were freed.

Act out a *scene* from your favorite movie. But for a funny twist, try to work the word *gold* into the dialogue. Take the famous line from *Forest Gump*: "Life is like a box of chocolates." Well, what if life were like a box of golden raisins? That wouldn't be quite as good, would it? But reciting this version could help you remember to associate the word *SCENE* with the Gold Rush. In fact, the word *scene* should make you think of movies, which should make you think of Hollywood, which is in California, which is where the California Gold Rush took place, of course. Is that a stretch?

Events Leading to the Civil War

▶ SWAB the DECK

Many different events led to the **U.S. Civil War.** Some laws that were passed by the federal government angered the North or the South. Sometimes a violent act committed against the North or the South increased the tension between the two regions. The capital letters in the acronym "SWAB the DECK" stand for the eight different events that eventually led to the Civil War.

Note that the word *the* is included only so that the mnemonic makes sense. Sailors on a ship are often ordered to "swab the deck." This means that they are supposed to clean the floor of the ship.

The following are eight events that led to the Civil War.

- **Sumner was caned:** In 1856, Charles Sumner, a senator, was attacked in Congress for speaking out against proslavery radicals.
- **Wilmot Proviso:** A proposed law that would have outlawed slavery in any new territories, but was never passed
- **Attack on Harper's Ferry:** John Brown attacked the Harper's Ferry arsenal in a failed attempt to give guns to slaves in order to establish a protected colony for freed slaves in the mountains.
- **"Bleeding Kansas":** In the 1850s, the Kansas territory was the scene of a mini civil war over the issue of slavery.
- *Dred Scott v. Sandford*: This Supreme Court decision infuriated abolitionists by saying that slaves were not citizens.
- **Election of 1860:** When Abraham Lincoln was elected president, it was the last straw for the Southern states that then decided to secede, or pull out.
- **Compromise of 1850:** An agreement neither side supported relating to the status of California and future western territories
- **Kansas-Nebraska Act:** This act put an end to the Missouri Compromise and opened the way for future territories to become slave states.

IT'S YOUR TURN

Write the acronym "SWAB the DECK" on a piece of paper. Remember that "the" in the middle is not part of the acronym. After studying the list for several minutes, see how many key events you can name based on the first letters. While the word *civil* in Civil War means "among citizens," the word *civil* can also mean "polite." So, you could imagine that a civil war should be fought on a clean surface. In order for that to happen, they'd have to SWAB the DECK!

The Golden Spike and the Transcontinental Railroad

▶ After the Golden Spike,
no one had to hike.
By 1869,
cross-country travel was just fine.

After the Civil War, train companies raced to lay their tracks across the country to create a **transcontinental railroad.** The nation's newspapers covered the heated competition on their front pages. The Central Pacific hurdled east from California, while the Union Pacific sped west from Nebraska. In order to win, both companies overworked freed slaves and immigrant laborers from China and Ireland.

On May 10, 1869, in Promontory Point, Utah, the rail tracks from the west met with the tracks from the east. Amid champagne toasts, the companies' chief engineers hammered in the Golden Spike, officially joining the lines.

You can use this rhyme to remember the year that construction of the transcontinental railroad was completed.

How many songs can you think of about trains? Maybe you're familiar with the traditional song "I've Been Working on the Railroad," "Take the Last Train to Clarksville" by the Monkees, or "The Loco-motion" by Little Eva. Try singing the rhyming lines of this mnemonic to the tune of any of these songs. You can even write additional lyrics for your song based on the information in the paragraphs above.

Causes of U.S. Industrial Growth

Between 1850 and 1900, the United States experienced an enormous increase in the number of manufactured goods produced each year. Many people believe that the invention of new **machines** was the reason. But many other factors played a part in the industrial growth.

The United States was a huge area of land and **natural resources** seemed to be in endless supply. The construction of **railroads** to transport these supplies and the finished products made production flow faster and easier.

The immense U.S. **population growth** during this period meant there were more consumers to buy the manufactured goods. A considerable number of people who caused the population growth were **immigrants** looking for work in the United States. Both skilled and unskilled workers were needed for the many new jobs being created.

Finally, an increased supply of money was available to new businesses. The early success of factories resulted in banks **lending** out money to businesses.

► You can help yourself remember the six reasons that industrialization was so successful in the United States by chunking the information into three categories.

Technologies	"People" factors	Resources
• machines	• population growth	• natural resources
• railroads	• immigrants seeking jobs	• lending/capital for businesses

Turn-of-the-Century Inventions

During the Second Industrial Revolution, advances in technology led to greater production and economic growth. In 1876, Alexander Graham Bell patented the **telephone,** and three years later, Thomas Edison invented the first usable **electric lightbulb.** To replace the steam engine, inventors developed a smaller engine that would run on gasoline, called the **internal combustion engine.** In 1888, George Eastman developed the **Kodak,** the first practical, handheld, point-and-shoot camera.

After the telephone, inventors sought to transmit messages without wires, using radio waves. A man named Guglielmo Marconi used the first successful **wireless telegraph** to send signals through the air. In 1903, the Wright brothers launched the first powered and sustained **airplane** flight, which lasted all of twelve seconds! And finally, Henry Ford made automobiles affordable for the average person by building them from standard parts, using an efficient process—the **assembly line.** The first of these cars was called the **Model T.**

> ### IT'S YOUR TURN
>
> Imagine you need to buy all the items on the following list of school supplies. You're afraid you'll lose the supply sheet—your backpack is like the Bermuda Triangle! So you decide to memorize the list.
>
> • loose leaf paper
> • graph paper
> • protractor
> • black ballpoint pens
> • colored pencils
> • index cards
> • no. 2 pencils
> • ruler
> • calculator
> • three-ring binder
> • highlighter
> • composition notebook
>
> Chunk the list into any categories you choose. For example, you may want to group writing tools together. Then, close your book and see how many of the 12 items you can remember.

▶ In order to memorize the inventions from 1876 to 1914, chunk the information into two categories.

Four "everyday use" inventions:
- telephone
- lightbulb
- Kodak box camera
- wireless telegraph

Four inventions relating to automobiles/transportation:
- internal combustion engine
- airplane
- Model T Ford
- assembly line

Roosevelt Corollary

▶ The Roosevelt "Corral-ary"

In 1904, Latin American countries were not very stable. The United States did not want Europe to sweep in and try to take over. Trade and business in Latin America was a large source of income for the United States, and the country wanted to protect those interests. The Monroe Doctrine in 1823 had established that any act against Latin America would be considered an act against the United States. **The Roosevelt Corollary** stated that the United States would not tolerate *any* interference in Latin America. It implied that the United States would not only watch Latin America closely, but also step in and take action whenever they felt it was needed.

The Roosevelt Corollary was a very significant message to the rest of the world. It showed that the United States was willing to declare and defend its interests. The Roosevelt Corollary was used for many years to justify U.S. actions in Latin America.

The keyword Roosevelt "Corral-ary" can help you remember the purpose of the Roosevelt Corollary. The word *corral* means to enclose people or things in a region that you can control. It's often used to describe a fenced-in area in which farmers keep their livestock. If you think about it, the United States was really attempting to corral Latin America—keeping others out of the enclosed area and protecting the resources inside for itself.

66 *Get This...*

Quick: What letter in the alphabet comes after *K*? Did you know the answer right away? Don't be discouraged if you didn't. Even adults often use a rhyming mnemonic to remember alphabetical order. The alphabet song we all learned in kindergarten is actually a mnemonic. It splits the letters of the alphabet into groups, and the last letters of the groups form a rhyme pattern. Many people know the alphabet song so well that they can recite a small part of it if you give them any starting letter. This just goes to show that mnemonics are tools for life. 99

Calvin Coolidge and Laissez-Faire Economics

▶ "Let's say . . . fair!"

Have you ever heard the expression, "All's fair in love and war"? Well, in laissez-faire economics, all's fair in business too. **Laissez-faire** (lā′-sā′-fer) is a French term that basically means "let them do what they want." The keywords "Let's say . . . fair!" sound similar to the pronunciation of *laissez-faire*. They also express the way **President Calvin Coolidge** (1923–1929) believed the government should handle business in the United States.

Coolidge believed that businesses should be left to their own controls without government interference. Coolidge felt that business was designed to benefit the community within which it existed. If there were any complaints about unfair business practices, Coolidge's response was that it *was* fair and that things would work themselves out.

In the late 1920s, business in the United States did prosper greatly, but not for everyone. Farmers were producing too much extra food. They couldn't sell it all and had to accept low prices for what they did sell. When the Congress tried to pass a law that would help out the farmers, Coolidge vetoed it. He felt that what the farmers were going through was a fair and natural part of capitalism. Many people believe that this philosophy led to the Great Depression in the United States.

Imagine that you are Calvin Coolidge. Have a friend present a list of complaints about unfair business practices. For each complaint on the list, they should stop and ask you, the president, whether that business practice is fair or unfair. Respond in your best presidential accent, "Hmm, let's say . . . fair!" For example, your friend might say, "John Rockefeller owns all the oil, so he is able to charge very high prices. Is this fair or unfair?" You know how to respond.

Cold War Crises of the Kennedy Administration

The **Cold War** was the period of hostility between communist countries and noncommunist Western countries that lasted from about 1946 to 1989.

During John F. Kennedy's presidency, there were three main events that symbolized the continuing conflict between the United States and the world's communist nations. Each of these events was a crisis that threatened to escalate the tensions to an all-out war.

The first crisis was the **Bay of Pigs** invasion in April 1961. It was an invasion by U.S. troops designed to overthrow Fidel Castro. Castro was the communist leader of Cuba. The invasion failed, and tensions between the United States and the Soviet Union, a communist ally of Cuba, increased.

This led to the second crisis. Because the United States was clearly willing to launch attacks against communism, the Soviet Union decided to block off the communist area of East Germany. In August 1961, the Soviet Union built the **Berlin Wall,** separating East Berlin from West Berlin. This move also prevented East Germans who did not want to live under communist rule from escaping.

The third crisis of the Cold War during Kennedy's presidency was the **Cuban missile crisis** of October 1962. Castro had asked the Soviet Union for more weapons to defend against America. Kennedy ordered a blockade to stop Soviet ships from delivering missiles to Cuba. The Soviets agreed to turn back, but only after the United States promised not to invade Cuba again.

▶ *One* rhymes with *bun*. A pig eating a bun tells me the Bay of Pigs invasion came first.

Two rhymes with *shoe*. A wall made of shoes tells me the construction of the Berlin Wall came second.

Three rhymes with *tree*. A tree full of missiles tells me that the Cuban missile crisis came third.

The Gulf of Tonkin Resolution

In the summer of 1964, North Vietnamese torpedo boats supposedly began firing on the United States' vessels in the Gulf of Tonkin, between Vietnam and China. It was unclear at the time (and still is, to some degree) if the attacks were legitimately launched by the Vietnamese. Nonetheless, President Lyndon B. Johnson used them as an excuse to escalate the United States' military involvement in Asia. The Gulf of Tonkin Resolution authorized the president to "take all necessary measures" to prevent more violence in the region.

"Tonkin" sounds like "honkin'," the sound a general might make with his tank while impatiently waiting to invade a country. So, to remember this important turning point in the Vietnam War, just imagine an anxious LBJ honkin' on the horn while preparing to attack in the Gulf of Tonkin.

▶ "Honkin' into Tonkin"

The Great Society Acts

▶ If I had to **vote** for the least **civil** of all the **medical** professionals I have ever known, it would definitely be the school nurse I had in **elementary school**. She never smiled!

Between 1964 and 1965, **President Lyndon B. Johnson** wished to take actions to improve civil rights and fight poverty. He believed that the United States could not be considered a "great society" unless they protected the poor, the minorities, and the children of the country. His **Great Society program** was made up of four different acts that were passed by Congress. The highlighted words in the chaining icon stand for the four different acts that made up Johnson's Great Society program:

• **Voting Rights Act**

In 1965, there were still many discriminatory election practices in place. The Voting Rights Act eliminated some of these practices by outlawing literacy tests as a voting requirement and ensuring more federal control over state and local voting regulations.

• **Civil Rights Act**

The Civil Rights Act of 1964 sought to reduce racial discrimination by banning discrimination in public facilities, public education, and federally funded programs. This act also established the Commission on Equal Employment Opportunity.

• **Medical Care Act**

The Medical Care Act of 1965 established the Medicare program, which provides health insurance for senior citizens.

• **Elementary and Secondary Education Act**

The Elementary and Secondary Education Act of 1965 sought to improve the academic achievement of disadvantaged students by funding education programs in poor communities. This act marked the beginning of the Head Start preschool program for children of low-income families.

IT'S YOUR TURN

Reread the chaining sentences. This time, as you read, imagine yourself actually filling out a ballot to vote for your elementary school nurse as the least polite person who has ever treated you when you were sick. Imagine sitting in the office of this sour-faced nurse, looking around at all of the medical supplies, including the peroxide that she dumps right on your cuts so they burn. Really cement the sentence in your brain. Then, close the book and test yourself on the four acts. Tonight, as you're going to sleep, see if you can still remember. Then, test yourself a week from now. It's important to keep reviewing your memory so that the information isn't lost.

Henry Kissinger: An American Statesman

▶ "KISSinger" and make up!

In 1968, President Nixon appointed **Henry Kissinger** as his national security adviser. Kissinger later served as Secretary of State. He was a skilled diplomat, and he made great strides toward making peace between the United States and several hostile communist countries, including North Vietnam, the Soviet Union, and China.

Kissinger won a Nobel Peace Prize in 1973 for his involvement in negotiating an end to the Vietnam War. In addition, he is credited for relaxing Cold War tensions between the United States and the Soviet Union throughout the 1970s. Finally, Kissinger paved the way for Nixon to visit and speak with the leader of China. This one visit had enormous effects for America and the rest of the world. China agreed to keep diplomatic talks open and to begin trading with America.

Note that, while this mnemonic highlights Kissinger's positive contributions to keeping international peace, Kissinger's foreign-policy legacy is controversial. He is criticized by historians for his roles in what many consider war crimes and human rights violations, including the bombing of neutral Cambodia during the Vietnam War and the assassinations of political opponents in Latin America.

Repeat the keyword phrase *loudly* many times. Eventually, your parents may ask you what on earth you are doing! Won't they be impressed when you tell them that you're just thinking about former Secretary of State Henry Kissinger. Next, ask them if they can do an impression of Henry Kissinger so that you will know what he sounded like. They probably can't match how deep and raspy Kissinger's voice is, but it's fun to hear them try!

The Bill of Rights

▶ "I'm home from school!" I shout. And as I walk through the *front door*, I'm thinking, "Finally, I can **speak freely** without having to worry about getting in trouble with my teacher." I see that my sister is already home because she has hung up her sweater in the *closet*, which reminds me that it's warm in here and I want to **bare my arms** too. I throw off my backpack and jacket and move down the *hall*, where my little brother has left toy **soldiers** lying out, again. I call out his name but he doesn't respond, so I go to **search** for him in *his bedroom*. "Mickey, where are you?" I call out, as I walk toward the *family room*. "There you are, parked in front of the television," I say. "Shh, I'm watching *Jeopardy*," he whines, which is odd, considering he's only five years old.

The first ten Amendments to the U.S. Constitution are called the **Bill of Rights.** The highlighted words in this story stand for the first five Amendments. Each of the italic words is a specific location that you can associate with one of the Amendments. As you read, you should visualize yourself physically walking through the surroundings that are described and experiencing the events in the order in which they occur.

The following are Amendments 1–5 of the Bill of Rights, paraphrased:

1. **Freedom of speech, religion, press, and assembly**

2. **Right to bear arms**

3. **No soldiers quartered in houses during peacetime**

4. **No unreasonable search and seizure**

5. **No double jeopardy** (citizens cannot be tried for the same crime twice), **and due process**

. . . .
It's Your Turn

Think of a class you have in school that has assigned seating. Try listing every student in the class based on the order in which their desks are arranged. Start with the person in the back left of the room and move right, or start with your own seat and move outward. See how long it takes you to name everyone using this technique, and check to make sure you didn't leave anyone off of the list. You're using the loci technique!

What Makes a Civilization?

▶ I still remember my first summer visiting the big **city** in 1945. My family and I went to a street fair where **skilled workers** were selling their wares. At one of the booths, an excited man was showing off his new **invention**. It was an amazing **writing** tool—you didn't have to fill it with lead or ink and it worked from gravity! He called it a ballpoint pen. The people gathered around were looking at this ink-stained man like he belonged in a mental **institution**, but I thought he was a genius.

The first human civilization was in ancient Sumer. (The phrase "first summer" in the first sentence will help you remember.) A civilization is more than just a large group of people who live in the same area. There are five major factors that determine whether a community is considered a civilization. The highlighted words in this story stand for the five different characteristics of a civilization.

A group of people living in the same geographic area is called a civilization if all of the following are present:

1. Developed **cities** that are centers for trade

2. **Workers** who have specialized skills

3. New **inventions** and improvements in technology

4. A developed alphabet and **system of writing**

5. **Institutions** such as schools, hospitals, and governments

Read the story aloud to yourself or to someone else who is willing to listen! When you reach one of the highlighted words, say it loudly. Try to think of the way each feature helps make a civilization.

Civic Duties

▶ **P**eter's **o**ldest **d**aughter **s**eizes **j**umping **v**iolets.

As citizens of our country we have both rights and responsibilities. Responsibilities are actions that all good citizens should perform. An adult's primary citizenship responsibilities are **paying taxes, obeying laws, defending the country, staying informed, jury duty**, and **voting.**

This acrostic sentence will help you remember the responsibilities of adult citizens. The first letter of each word in the sentence stands for one responsibility. For example, the *P* in *Peter* reminds you of the responsibility to *pay* taxes, and so on.

. . . .
IT'S YOUR TURN

Making up an acrostic sentence can help you remember any list of things. Try making up an acrostic sentence to help you remember the five basic freedoms granted to U.S. citizens by the First Amendment: freedom of *religion*, freedom of *speech*, freedom of the *press*, freedom of peaceable *assembly*, and freedom to *petition the government for change.*

Lobbying

Lobbyists are private citizens who attempt to influence the government's decisions. There are several different types of lobbyists. **Grassroots lobbyists** try to bring about change by stirring up the public through local campaigns.

Public interest groups are organizations that attempt to protect the public by ensuring that the government is acting in their best interests. For example, a public interest group may act as a watchdog for environmental issues or it may advocate on behalf of consumers.

A company might hire **corporate lobbyists** to convince the government to pass laws that will benefit that company. For example, advocates for pharmaceutical corporations may lobby Congress for legislation that will make it easier to get a new drug approved.

Various lobbying groups sponsor **think tanks** to do their research for them. A think tank is a privately funded (usually) research group, comprised of academics or experts in a field, that attempts to shape government policy.

▶ Create a flash card for each type of lobby group and put the cards in places that you can associate with the group.
- Make a "grassroots" card and tape it onto the front of a potted plant (or in your front yard).
- A "public interest group" card can go atop a clipboard or notepad.
- A "corporate lobbyists" card can go on top of a jar of pennies, a checkbook, or a wallet.
- A card for "think tank" can be taped to a clear bowl or a fish tank.

Arrange all of these items in the "lobby" of your house. Pretend you are a senator and all of the lobbyists are trying to give you money to pass a bill. Argue with them at length until you can persuade your mother's petunias that they are wrong!

Congress

The United States legislature, also known as **Congress,** is our country's lawmaking body. Because our Congress has two separate houses, it is considered a *bicameral* legislature. The two houses are the Senate and the House of Representatives. In order for a bill to be passed, it has to be approved by both houses.

The **Senate** has **100 members,** 2 from each state. The vice president is the official leader of the Senate and has the power to cast a tiebreaking vote. The Senate has the power to impeach government officials (charge them with a crime). The Senate also has the power to approve cabinet appointments, Supreme Court nominees, and treaties. A senator serves a 6-year term and must be at least 30 years old to be elected.

Use the following mnemonic to remember the number of senators in the Senate.

► The prefix *cent–* means "one hundred," and there are 100 "cent"-ators in the Senate.

The **House of Representatives** has **435 members,** and each member represents a certain district. Representatives are supposed to voice the views of the people they represent, who are known as their *constituents*. The number of representatives a state has depends on its population. California has 53 representatives, while tiny Rhode Island has just 2. A member of the House of Representatives serves a 2-year term and must be at least 25 years old to be elected.

66 *Get This . . .*

The number of representatives in the House of Representatives changes with the population changes in the United States. After the census is held at the end of each decade, the number of representatives changes accordingly. So, you might have to come up with a new mnemonic in 2011! **99**

To remember the number of representatives in the House, think of a way to put the numbers 4, 3, and 5 in the right order.

► My local representative asked for a campaign contribution, so I reached into my wallet **for three five**-dollar bills.

Ancient Greek Civilization

The **Ancient Greek civilization** lasted from about 2000 B.C. until 150 B.C. During this period, the Greeks experienced four different ages.

▶ The first age (remember *one* rhymes with *bun*) was the **Bronze Age**.

The Bronze Age
2000 – 1150 B.C.

The Bronze Age lasted more than 800 years, from 2000 B.C. until 1150 B.C. The Greek city-states fought many wars during this time, against both each other and foreign enemies. They also developed arts and government as important parts of their civilization.

The second age (remember *two* rhymes with *shoe*) was known as the **Dark Ages**.

The Dark Ages
1150 – 750 B.C.

Historians are "in the dark" about much of what occurred during the Dark Ages. Brutal wars and less advanced people caused the Greeks to lose the art of writing, so almost no records were kept about this time period. The Dark Ages lasted about 400 years, from 1150 B.C. until 750 B.C.

The third age (remember *three* rhymes with *tree*) was the **Golden Age**.

The Golden Age began slowly. Greeks were starting to try to act more like the heroes of their history and theater. They wished to achieve excellence, both in body and mind. The Olympics began near the beginning of the Golden Age. Philosophy and drama were also results of the Golden Age, which lasted from 750 B.C. to 323 B.C.

The Golden Age
750 – 323 B.C.

The **Hellenistic Age** was the fourth age of Ancient Greek civilization. (Remember that *four* rhymes with *door*.)

The Hellenistic Age lasted from 323 B.C. until 150 B.C. During this age there were many advances in mathematics, science, and sculpture. The concept of pi, the actual size of Earth, and the lever were all discoveries made during this age.

. . . .
IT'S YOUR TURN

Cover this page with a sheet of paper and see if you can name all four ages by recalling the images.

The Hellenistic Age
323 – 150 B.C.

Greek Philosophers

▶ SPA

The Greeks invented the art of *philosophy,* a word which means "the love of wisdom." The acronym SPA is a useful way of remembering the order in which the three leading Greek philosophers became popular. **Socrates** was the first. He is often considered the father of philosophy. **Plato** was a student of Socrates who believed that our senses can deceive us and that reality can be known only through rational thought. **Aristotle** was a student of Plato who believed that knowledge came from experience.

The acronym SPA is an easy mnemonic for recalling which philosopher came first, but sometimes you need a way to remember the acronym! Picture three men in togas sitting in a hot spring. The first man could have an "S" on his toga. The next guy could have a "P" on his toga, and the third man could wear an "A" on his toga. When you need to remember who taught who, just imagine these three men philosophizing in a spa.

The Roman Republic

▶ **P**asta **c**ookers **s**haped **m**odern **d**emocracy.

A republic is a state in which the government's power rests on the consent of the people. The **Roman Republic** was founded in 510 B.C. and lasted almost 500 years. The principles of the Roman republic and the (slightly earlier) Athenian democracy later formed the basis of modern democracies like the United States. The first letter in each word of this acrostic stands for one branch of this Roman government.

People: The common people, known as *plebeians,* had the least power at first. As Rome grew and more commoners were recruited into the military, the power of the people grew as well. The citizen assembly was given the power to make laws beginning in 287 B.C.

Consuls: The two consuls were the chief magistrates. They had much of the power in the government, as they were the leaders of the Senate. However, they could overrule each other's decisions, and they could serve only one-year terms.

Magistrates: Magistrates are public officials. Other Roman magistrates included *quaestors* (who ran the treasury), *aediles* (who maintained public buildings and festivals), *praetors* (who were like junior consuls), and census officials.

Senate: The senate was a large group of mostly upper-class citizens. The senators' opinions strongly influenced government policy, although technically they did not have much authority. Senators served lifelong terms.

Dictator: The dictator was an emergency ruler who would be chosen by the consuls. He would have absolute power for a short period of time (usually only when Rome was threatened with invasion).

❝ *Get This . . .*

Referring to Italians as "pasta cookers" borders on politically incorrect. But many people find it easier to recall mnemonics that are offensive, crude, or even gory. You've probably heard the story about King Henry VIII of England and his six wives. Did you know that there's a mnemonic for remembering the fates of his six wives?

This unpleasant verse goes "divorced, beheaded, died, divorced, beheaded, survived." That's right, Henry VIII had not one, but *two* of his wives beheaded on the accusation that they had been unfaithful to him (although it's more likely that he really had them killed because they didn't bear him any male offspring). How's that for crude? **❞**

The Spread of Christianity from 300–450

▶ GABE'S JIGS

During the years 300–450, the Roman Empire was in a state of decline. This opened the way for the rapid spread of Christianity. Before the year 300, Christianity was popular in many areas that the apostle Paul had visited. He had introduced Christianity throughout the eastern Mediterranean and many groups of people found it appealing. Women and the poor, particularly, found Christianity to be a welcome change.

The spread of Christianity between 300 and 450 was remarkable. For example, in Spain, only a small part of the southern region was Christian in 300. By 450, the entire country had been exposed to Christianity. This phenomenon occurred in many countries during this relatively short 150-year span.

- **Gaul**
- **Asia Minor**
- **Britain**
- **Egypt**
- **Syria**
- **Judea**
- **Italy**
- **Greece**
- **Spain**

Each letter in the acronym above stands for one of the nine territories Christianity spread into between 300 and 450.

In Christianity, Gabriel is an archangel. To help you remember the acronym GABE'S JIGS, pretend you are an angel by holding out your arms like wings. Now, try to do an Irish jig while flapping your wings. This action will not only imprint the acronym on your brain, but also help you remember that the acronym has to do with the spread of Christianity.

Meso-American Civilizations

► Oh, my tender tooth aches!

This acrostic tells you the major **civilizations** that inhabited what is now **Mexico** from about 1200 B.C. to the late 1500s. The first letter (or first two letters) of each word in the sentence stands for one of these civilizations. This acrostic also presents these civilizations roughly in the order in which they thrived. Note that the Teotihuacán civilization existed at the same time as the Mayan civilization. These two cultures were aware of each other and often traded.

Olmec: The Olmec thrived in Mesoamerica from about 500 B.C.–300 B.C. The Olmec were the major civilization of the Pre-Classic period and are sometimes referred to as the "Mother Culture" of Middle America. They were the first to use stone for architectural monuments.

Maya: Although the Maya had settled as early as 1500 B.C., the height of Mayan culture was from about 200 A.D. to 900 A.D. The Maya and the Teotihuacán were the major civilizations of the Classic period. The Maya developed a hieroglyphic system for writing and a calendar.

Teotihuacán: The Teotihuacán settled around 1 A.D. and thrived from about 200 A.D. to 650 A.D. The Teotihuacán were the first truly urban civilization in Mesoamerica with a population of nearly 125,000 at one time.

It's Your Turn

You can create your own acrostic mnemonic to remember the names and order of these Mexican civilizations. Try to think of a memorable four-word sentence. The words should begin with the letters *O, M, Te, To* and *A*. Some examples include "Old men tend to amble," or "Order me ten toasted appetizers." Remember, anything that will stick with you is a good mnemonic device. After you come up with your own sentence, close the book and test yourself to see if you can remember the names of the major Mexican civilizations.

Toltec: The Toltec were a major Mesoamerican civilization of the Post-Classic period from about 1000 A.D. The Toltec were a practical, warlike people who are known for their monuments made from severed human heads.

Aztec: The Aztec formed a mighty empire in what is now Mexico, where they flourished from about 1200 A.D. to 1600 A.D. Much of their prosperity was due to their advanced agricultural systems. The Aztec capital of Tenochtitlán (which is now Mexico City) was one of the greatest cities in the world at the time the Spanish conquered Mexico.

The Huns

▶ Hun-y, you shrunk the Gupta.

The Mongolians were a warlike people who roamed Asia in large tribes. One of these tribes was known as the **Huns.** You may have heard of their infamously cruel king, Attila the Hun. The Huns relentlessly attacked India from the 400s to the 600s. During this time, the mighty **Gupta Empire in India** was severely weakened. The different areas of land that made up their empire grew smaller.

Often, a strange visual image will really reinforce a keyword mnemonic. The picture below shows a Hun aiming a shrink ray at the Taj Mahal, the famous Indian monument. Even though the Huns predated the Taj Mahal by more than 1,000 years, the building is a widely recognized symbol of Indian culture. And the picture of Attila the Hun wielding a shrink ray is just odd enough to be memorable!

Chinese Inventions

▶ Always remember to bring your **compass** on your travels so you won't get lost after escaping from the **gunpowder**-toting wild men you read about in the stories they **print** in the tabloids.

The T'ang and Sung dynasties ruled China for over 600 years, from about 618 to 1279. At the height of this epoch, three different inventions were created and developed. The highlighted words in this chaining mnemonic represent these major advances that impacted the entire world.

The **magnetic compass** revolutionized travel on land and at sea. It is believed that **gunpowder** was first used in fireworks in the 600s. It was mainly used to create dazzling light shows during celebrations. Four hundred years later, the Chinese created stronger concentrations of gunpowder that could be used as weapons. The discovery of gunpowder changed the face of warfare. Finally, the technique of **printing** using wood blocks originated in China more than 800 years before Gutenberg invented the printing press.

Draw a picture to help you remember this chaining mnemonic. Try to make it look exaggerated, like the cover of a tabloid magazine. You may want to draw yourself running through the wilderness, trying to read a compass. In the background, draw a Bigfoot (the tabloid magazines' favorite subject) holding a firecracker. The more outrageous your drawing is, the better you will remember the details from the sentence.

Chinese Influence on Japanese Culture

▶ Japan and China: **BIG WAR** from 500 to 800

Japan is an island and it is very mountainous. These geographic features protected Japan from invasion by the more powerful China; thus, Japan and China didn't engage in an *actual* war from 500 to 800. But while the Japanese were capable of remaining independent from China, they did borrow many of China's ideas and institutions.

The letters in the acronym BIG WAR stand for different things that Japan borrowed from Chinese culture between the years 500 and 800. B is for **building styles,** IG is for **imperial government,** W is for **writing styles,** A is for **art forms,** and R is for **religion.** All of these aspects of Japanese culture were influenced by Chinese culture. Japan actually sent scholars to China to learn art techniques, forms of governing, and religious practice.

❝ *Get This...*

There is an urban myth that the word *news* is actually an acronym. You may have heard that *news* was originally made up from the first letters of North, East, West, and South. This isn't actually true. Although it would be a very clever acronym (because news is information that comes from all directions) the word *news* in the sense of "recent events" has been in use since the fifteenth century. **❞**

The Five Pillars of Islam

▶ **Pious followers achieve Five Pillars.**

This acrostic helps you remember the **Five Pillars of Islam.** The Five Pillars of Islam are the different acts that Muslims must carry out. The first letter of each word in the acrostic stands for one of the Five Pillars of Islam. Remember that *pious* is another word for religious.

The Five Pillars of Islam are:

Prayer: Muslims must recite five daily prayers at specific times of day.

Faith: Muslims must proclaim a belief in Allah (God) and the prophet Muhammad.

Alms: Muslims must donate a certain percentage of their savings to the poor.

Fasting: During the holy month of Ramadan, healthy adult Muslims may not eat or drink from dawn to dusk.

Pilgrimage: Once in a lifetime, a Muslim should make a pilgrimage to the holy city of Mecca.

The fact that the words "Five Pillars" are part of the acrostic will help you remember the mnemonic. Also, the sentence actually describes something about the topic. It tells you that devoted Muslims follow the Five Pillars.

Another unique aspect of this acrostic is that the letters PFAFP form a palindrome. That means the letters are the same forward and backward. This can help you remember if you forget one of the words.

The Holy Roman Emperor

▶ Charlemagne shared the fame.

In the year 800, **Charlemagne** was the king of Western Europe. He was extremely popular and powerful as well. Knowing this, **Pope Leo III** asked Charlemagne to visit him in Rome. He crowned Charlemagne and named him the **Holy Roman Emperor.**

This new title did not give Charlemagne any new power. Instead, it gave the Roman Church more power and fame because people saw the church as being connected to the powerful king of Western Europe. By giving Charlemagne a crown and a title, the church looked like it was responsible for choosing the emperor. In fact, the church later played an important role in choosing emperors.

There are three syllables in the keywords "shared the fame" and in the name Charlemagne. Keep repeating "Charlemagne," and clap three times, once for each syllable. Do the same for "shared the fame." Next, put them both together. Clapping for every syllable will help you keep the phrase in your head.

Farming Advances in the High Middle Ages

▶ If you want to **plow** through a marathon, you should eat like a **horse** the night before (especially carbs, like pasta), you should **harness** all your energy by getting plenty of rest the week before, and you should build up some muscle over the preceding months by running laps around the **three fields** behind the school.

One feature that set the High Middle Ages apart from the Middle Ages was advances in farming. New tools and techniques enabled farmers to produce more food and farm more land in less time. The highlighted words in this chaining mnemonic represent **advances in farming in the High Middle Ages.**

The following advances in farming were part of the reason Europe flourished during the High Middle Ages.

- The **heavy plow** allowed farmers to make better use of the soil, which resulted in better crops.
- Using **horses** instead of oxen allowed farmers to farm much more land in a day.
- The **new harnesses** used on horses stopped choking them, allowing horses to work harder and longer.
- The **three-field system** divided up land into sections that rotated in and out of use, allowing the unused soil to renew itself. This allowed farmers to use more of their land each year and resulted in better crops.

When reading the sentence, act out the three steps you need to take in order to "plow" through a marathon. For example, pretend you're eating a big bowl of pasta the night before the race. Maybe you're eating greedily, like a horse. Or maybe you're bending over your bowl, pretending to eat the pasta out of a trough. Take in all the calories you can—you have an imaginary twenty-six-mile race tomorrow!

The Magna Carta

▶ When King John signed the Magna Carta,
it made his life a little harder.
The limited power of the British king
began that day in 1215.

The **Magna Carta** was a very important document. It forever changed the way people thought of the British monarchy. It introduced new ideas that limited the power of the government, such as the right to a trial by jury and the idea of no taxation without representation. The Declaration of Independence of the United States was influenced by the Magna Carta.

King John was forced to sign the Magna Carta by the British nobles who were tired of his failed attempts to win land from France. By signing the Magna Carta, John agreed that a king also had to follow the laws and customs of the land.

Repeat the poem to yourself a few times. The word *harder* kind of rhymes with *Carta*, but it does not rhyme perfectly. It may help you to remember the poem if you use a tough-guy accent and pronounce the word *harder* as if it were spelled "hardah." Repeat the poem again using this new pronunciation. Does that help you remember the poem? Sometimes a small flaw or a quirk in a mnemonic can actually help you remember it better.

The Spanish Inquisition

▶ Besides helping Columbus to sail the ocean blue,
we have some other, more troubling news.
Also in the year 1492,
Isabel and Ferdinand ousted the Jews.

Many people use a cute little rhyme to help them remember that, in 1492, Christopher Columbus made his famous voyage to America. Most people also know that Queen Isabella I and King Ferdinand II of Spain paid for this voyage. This mnemonic turns that cute rhyme on its head, reminding us of the dark side of that period in Spanish history.

In 1492, the Catholic king and queen began a campaign known as the **Spanish Inquisition** against the Jews living in Spain. The goal was to convert all Jews to Christianity, so that Spain would be an all-Christian country. Most Jews were not willing to convert to Christianity. They were forced to leave Spain altogether, or else face torture and death. Some of the Jews who fled Spain actually traveled on the three boats Columbus took on his way to discovering America.

Pretend you are a news anchor reporting this information to your audience. This mnemonic is based on the well-known rhyme "In 1492, Columbus sailed the ocean blue." You can begin your report by telling how this mnemonic does not tell the whole story of what was happening in Spain in 1492.

The Beginnings of Protestantism

► Martin Luther simply could not sit still,
and listen to the immoral story
of a friar named Johann Tetzel,
who was selling pardons from Purgatory.

Martin Luther is most famous for writing his **95 Theses** and nailing the document to the door of a church in Germany. This paper attacked Catholic leaders for taking money from their followers in exchange for pardoning their sins. The idea was that those who paid for pardons would have to spend less time in Purgatory after they died before going to heaven.

A friar named Johann Tetzel went overboard in selling these pardons, called **indulgences.** He was so eager to collect the money, he would sell these indulgences no matter what sin the buyer had committed. Martin Luther saw this as an attempt to *sell* heaven. He felt this was an offense to his religion. His 95 Theses attacked the religious leaders who offered this deal and the pope who supported the practice. Luther's *protest* marked the beginning of **Protestantism,** which divided the Christian world.

❝ *Get This . . .*

Have you ever seen a television show in which a kid misbehaves in class and the teacher makes him stay after school and write "I will not use obscenities" one hundred times across the chalkboard? Well, staying after school and doing a repetitive task until your arm is about to fall off is certainly a form of punishment. But it may also be good for you.

Many people learn best when they rewrite their notes or sections of a textbook by hand. This study technique is called *transcription*. Writing the information helps them process it. And the more times they rewrite the text, the more likely they are to remember. So, even if the punishment doesn't help the kid in detention shape up, at least he'll never forget how to spell *obscenities!* ❞

The Enlightenment

▶ **R**easonably **n**ormal **h**andymen **p**atch **l**eaks.

In Europe during the 1700s, there were many advances in science, art, and philosophy. This period of thought and progress is known as the **Enlightenment.** A group of thinkers known as philosophers used a scientific approach to thinking about life. This method involved making observations and drawing logical conclusions.

The first letters of the words in the sentence above stand for the five main ideas of the Enlightenment. Also, the first word in the sentence includes the word *reason*, which is the central idea of the Enlightenment.

Below are the five main ideas of the Enlightenment:

Reason: Rational thought—not superstition, tradition, or emotion—is the path to knowledge and virtue.

Nature: The laws of nature are reasonable and the universe has order.

Happiness: Happiness is a human right. This was a revolutionary idea.

Progress: Society and individuals should strive to improve and grow.

Liberty: Individual freedoms lead to a society of advanced citizens.

The period of history that includes the Enlightenment is sometimes called the Age of Reason. To help you remember the acrostic, take a look at the comics on the next page. Pay attention to the details, such as the looks on the men's faces when they notice the flooding. Whose reaction seems more reasonable?

The Three Estates of France before the Revolution

From the Middle Ages until the French Revolution began in 1789, French society was divided into three social classes. These classes were known as the Three Estates. It was the way these different estates were treated that helped bring about the French Revolution.

The **First Estate** was made up of the Catholic clergy. The cross is a symbol of the church. Bishops, archbishops, and abbots profited greatly from their position in the First Estate. They paid no real taxes, but did offer the government a small portion of their yearly income.

The **Second Estate** was made up of the nobility of France. Try to associate the wealthy nobles with big fancy shoes. The nobles of France owned a huge portion of the land in France, but only made up a small part of the population. They did not pay taxes of any kind, even though they had the most money. This greatly angered members of the lowest social class.

The **Third Estate** was by far the largest class of French people. The commoners made up the Third Estate. They included farmers, the poor, and the working class. They paid almost all the taxes in France, and were required to work for the government without pay. Imagine all of France as a single tree. The Third Estate would be the roots, branches, and leaves of the tree. The other two estates might be the flowers on the tree.

▶ *One* rhymes with *bun*. A hamburger bun with a cross can help you remember that the Catholic clergy was the First Estate.

Two rhymes with *shoe*. A nobleman with fancy, oversized shoes can help you remember that the French nobility made up the Second Estate.

Three rhymes with *tree*. A poor farmer planting a tree can help you remember that the common people made up the Third Estate.

Push-Pull Factors for Immigration in the 1800s

▶ Pull-ups exercise flabby arms.
Push-ups increase really fit people's charms.

In the mid-1800s, people from all over Europe left their homes for the United States. There were many different factors that led people to immigrate to the U.S. These factors are usually split into two groups: "push" factors and "pull" factors. **Push factors** are reasons that people felt pushed out of their home countries. **Pull factors** are reasons that people felt pulled toward the United States. This acrostic represents all the main factors for immigration into the United States in the nineteenth century. And it rhymes!

Pull factors were desirable conditions that existed in the United States.

- **economic opportunity**
- **freedom**
- **abundant land**

Push factors were negative conditions in some European countries that caused people to leave.

- **Industrial Revolution** (factories decreased the need for artisans and skilled workers)
- **religious persecution** (several groups, including Jews from Germany and Quakers from Norway, were persecuted for their faith)
- **farming advances** (big farms with modern technologies put the small farms out of business)
- **population growth** (overcrowding in Europe caused food and job shortages)
- **crop failures** (failures of key crops caused food shortages)

It's time for some exercise! To help you remember this acrostic, act it out. Pretend to do pull-ups as you recite the first line of the acrostic. Then, drop to the floor and do five push-ups as you recite the second line—one push-up for each push factor in the acrostic.

Five Reasons Great Britain Led the Industrial Revolution

▶ SLING

The acronym SLING is a useful way of remembering the five factors that made Great Britain the leader in the Industrial Revolution. Each letter in SLING stands for a different factor that contributed to the mass production of goods. A sling supports an injured arm, helping it to heal. Similarly, the Industrial Revolution propped up Great Britain as a world superpower.

Stability was a key factor in creating an atmosphere of investing and inventing. Britain was involved in no wars during the Industrial Revolution, so merchants were less afraid of investing money.

This **lending** helped businesses prosper and helped fund the many new **inventions** that were such a huge part of the Industrial Revolution. Great Britain also enjoyed a large stock of **natural resources** required to run the machines. Water, iron ore, and coal were the three main resources required.

As an island, Great Britain was surrounded by harbors. This **geography** made trade with many other countries much easier.

Causes of World War I

▶ **MAIN** causes of World War I

The acronym MAIN is a useful way of remembering the four primary factors that led to World War I.

Militarism (the idea that a country should have a strong army and navy): Germany was building up its military, and Britain, who had traditionally had the strongest navy in the world, was feeling threatened.

Alliances (nations pledging support to each other, bound by their common distrust of other countries): As almost every nation had multiple alliances, any conflict was bound to become a worldwide affair. Leading up to World War I, the two main alliances were the Triple Alliance (Italy, Germany, and Austria-Hungary) and the Triple Entente (Great Britain, France, and Russia).

Imperialism (the idea that a powerful country should take control of smaller, weaker regions): The decline of the Ottoman Empire opened up the East to colonization, and European countries were fighting over African colonies too.

Nationalism (the idea that one's country is the best in the world and is worth fighting for): The Serbians wanted a Slavic national identity separate from Austro-Hungarian rule. Having lost territory in the Franco-Prussian War, the French nationalists wanted revenge. And the founding of the German Empire had created a strong sense of national pride among Germans.

In order to remember that the acronym MAIN stands for the causes of World War I, remember that World War I was one of the *main* events of the twentieth century for almost every world power. It was even called the Great War and the "war to end all wars," although of course we now know that wasn't true. To help you understand the impact of this war, consider that more than 15 million people lost their lives.

The Tropic of Cancer

▶ Raise your hand to answer,
Where's the tropic of Cancer?

Many people confuse the tropic of Cancer and the tropic of Capricorn. The **tropic of Cancer** is an imaginary line that runs around the Earth at 23.5 degrees north of the equator. It runs through Mexico, Egypt, and India.

The tropic of Capricorn is the imaginary line that runs around the Earth at 23.5 degrees south of the equator. It runs through Australia, Brazil, and South Africa.

The word *raise* in the rhyme will help you remember that the tropic of Cancer is *above* the equator. Where we live, in the Northern Hemisphere, the Sun is directly above the tropic of Cancer at noon on the first day of summer. This event is called the summer solstice.

. . . .
IT'S YOUR TURN

One way to keep busy and brush up on your geography skills during long car trips is to play geography games such as "I'm thinking of a country that starts with the letter *A*." How many countries can you think of that begin with the letter *A*?

Now, look at a world map and see how many countries you can find whose names start with *A*. Use mnemonics to remember the names of unfamiliar countries. For example, you might imagine a celebrity shopping for *antiques* with bodyguards (*armed men*) to remember Antigua and Armenia. After you study the map and create a few of your own mnemonics, play the game with a friend. One person may start by naming Australia, and then the other person might reply with America. Keep going until one player is stumped.

Longitude vs. Latitude

Longitude, latitude. Latitude, longitude. One means a distance north or south of the equator. The other means a distance east or west of the prime meridian. Put the two geographical terms together, and you can find any spot on the planet. But get them mixed up, and you might end up way, way off target. So how can you remember which is which?

The two terms are spelled nearly alike. But one starts with "long" and the other starts with "lat." Look at the diagram of longitude and latitude on the following page.

The lines of **longitude** run north-south from the North Pole to the South Pole. The lines of *longitude* are *always long*! The lines of **latitude** run from east to west. When they get close to the poles, they can get very small. The lines of latitude change size, depending on how far from the equator they are. Remember this, and you'll always remember that longitude lines are the consistently *long* lines on a map.

Some people get cranky when the weather gets too hot or too cold. If they flew north or south, maybe they could change their attitude. So you could say that they could change their attitude by changing their latitude. Remember this rhyme, and you'll always remember that latitude is the distance from the equator.

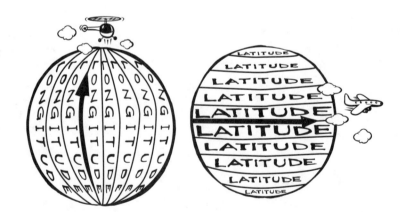

 Say the words *longitude* and *latitude* out loud, stressing the *loooong* part of *longitude* to reinforce that lines of longitude are always long.

The Nile River

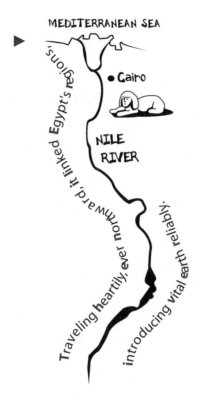

MEDITERRANEAN SEA

● Cairo

NILE RIVER

Traveling heartily, ever northward, it linked Egypt's regions, introducing vital earth reliably.

This acrostic provides important information about the **Nile River.** The Nile is a very strong river that flows northward from East Africa, through Egypt, and empties into the Mediterranean Sea. Ancient Egyptians worshipped the Nile for the many advantages it provided. They traveled on the river to other parts of Egypt. They also depended on the Nile to provide their dry land with new rich soil. Every year they could count on the Nile to flood around the same time. This flood would leave rich soil that helped grow crops. In an area with little rain and dry soil, the Nile River was a life-giving resource. It helped Egypt become a powerful civilization.

. . . .
It's Your Turn

Read the sentence to yourself several times. Next, on a sheet of paper, write out the letters in THE NILE RIVER from the top of the page to the bottom. Remember that each word in the sentence begins with the letters in THE NILE RIVER. Try to rewrite the sentence without looking. Once you can rewrite the sentence from memory, think about the information it provides.

The acrostic sentence gives information about the Nile River. And if you combine the first letters of each word in the sentence, they spell out "the Nile River." Pretty cool, huh?

Mesopotamia

▶ In between the Tigris and the Euphrates,
civilization began for men and ladies.

The first major civilization in human history began in the southwest part of Asia in a region called **Mesopotamia.** Because water was so important, the first cities always developed on coastlines, or near bodies of water. Most of Mesopotamia lay between two large rivers. These rivers are called the **Tigris River** and the **Euphrates River.**

After reading the rhyme a few times, find Mesopotamia on a map (today, most of this region is known as Iraq). Find the Tigris and Euphrates rivers, too, and notice how they surround the region. Try to imagine why being near a river was so important for the first civilizations. Keep in mind that there were no cars or trains. Remember that they did not have plumbing. Can you see how useful it would be to be close to a river?

The Indus-Ganges Plain

▶ "India's Candy Plain"

The **Indus-Ganges Plain** is a huge area of flat land in India. It is surrounded by the two rivers that make up its name. The Indus River and the Ganges River bring water to the plain. These rivers flowing into the heart of India create rich soil for growing crops, making those who live there very happy! It was this fertile land that enabled large civilizations to thrive as early as 2500 B.C.

Not only could the water from these rivers be used for drinking and watering crops, the rivers could also provide quicker, easier transportation. In the ancient world, civilizations could not survive without access to water and soil for growing food. An area of land surrounded by two large rivers could be assured of receiving a plentiful supply of water. In other words, the Indus-Ganges Plain was a pretty "sweet" place to live!

❝ *Get This . . .*

At thirteen years old, James Williams won the 2003 National Geographic Bee by answering the question "Goa, a state in southwestern India, was a possession of which country until 1961?" How on earth did he remember that? He had studied a map that showed all the territories belonging to different European superpowers in different colors. Goa was purple. He thought about it for a bit and then it came to him, "Purple is Portugal!" ❞

Isolated China

▶ DOME

The acronym DOME is a useful way of remembering four reasons that China was historically cut off from other cultures. Each letter in DOME stands for a different factor that caused China to be isolated. China was surrounded on all borders by different geographic obstacles. There were **deserts** to the north and west. To the east was the Pacific **Ocean**. South and west were huge **mountains** called the Himalayas. In addition, north of China was a people known as the Mongols, who did not wish friendly relations with other cultures (hence the label "**enemies**").

A dome is a protective shield that covers an area. Sports arenas sometimes have domes to keep out bad weather. Imagine a dome around China that kept out other cultures instead of rain.

You can create a simple model to help you remember these four factors. Imagine that the surface of a tabletop is China. On the left-most edge of the table, pour some sand to represent the desert (sugar will work in a pinch). On the right edge, pour a little water to symbolize the Pacific Ocean. At the bottom of the table, put a couple of upside-down ice-cream cones to represent tall mountains (chocolate morsels would work too). Finally, put some plastic army men at the top, to represent the enemies to the north. As you look around the table, remember what each material symbolizes.

State Capitals in New England

New England is the region in the northeastern United States that includes Maine, New Hampshire, Vermont, Massachusetts, Rhode Island, and Connecticut. Most people remember that Boston is the capital of Massachusetts, but they have trouble recalling some of the lesser-known New England state capitals.

That's where these mock bumper stickers come in. Have you ever read a silly bumper sticker—maybe something about whirled peas or beating up honor students—and it has stuck in your head much longer than you would have liked? Well, we hope these bumper stickers will stick with you because they can help you remember your state capitals. For example, while "I *'hart'* Connecticut" might seem like a moronic misspelling at first, in fact, it is intended to help you remember that Hartford is the capital of Connecticut.

. . . .
IT'S YOUR TURN

Draw a bumper sticker that could help someone remember the capital of the state in which you live. If you live in one of the New England states already shown, pick a state capital that you always forget and draw a bumper sticker that can help you remember in the future.

The state capitals represented by the bumper stickers are **Augusta, Maine; Concord, New Hampshire; Hartford, Connecticut;** and **Providence, Rhode Island** (although many people think that the entire state of Rhode Island is an island, most of the state is part of the mainland).

The Five Climatic Regions of Africa

► I decided to **coast** on my bike down the **grassy** hill toward the school playground so I could look for my friend **Savanna**. The playground was **desert**ed, probably because it was as hot and humid as a **rain forest** outside, so I decided to bike over to the public pool.

The African continent is made up of five different climatic regions. The highlighted words in the chaining mnemonic above represent the five different **regions of Africa**. Each region of Africa supports a different type of community.

Below is a list of the five regions of Africa and the type of population each one supports.

Coastland: The northern and southern coasts of Africa are small areas of land which support very large populations because they are near water.

Grassland: This dry grassy flatland supports smaller populations of farmers who let their livestock graze on the grasses.

Savanna: Huge areas of Africa are subtropical savannas, which have both rainy and dry seasons. Farmers can grow grain and rice here, but the soil is not of the best quality.

Desert: Huge areas of Africa are dry desert land, where there is little water except for small oases, where small groups of people live.

Rain forest: As the name suggests, the African rain forests are wet and heavily wooded. They do not support human communities very well because the insects carry diseases, but they support a wide variety of animal species.

On a sheet of construction paper, draw a large target with a bull's-eye and four rings surrounding it. Use colored pencil to shade each section with a different color. Then, use black marker to label each section of the target as one of the five different regions of Africa.

Ball up some small strips of paper. Recite the chaining mnemonic aloud. When you reach a highlighted word, try to hit the corresponding section of the target with a paper ball. Keep reciting the mnemonic over and over until you hit all five sections. The longer it takes, the less likely you are to forget!

GEOGRAPHY

The Oceans in Size Order

▶ Just remember, if you're preparing for a trip around the globe . . .
Pack an ocean **atl**as—it's an **ind**ispensable **article.**

Ocean water covers about 71 percent of the surface of the earth. The continents divide this water into four major oceans: the Pacific, the Atlantic, the Indian, and the Arctic. The mnemonic can help you remember the four oceans in size order, with the Pacific Ocean (represented by the word *Pack*) being the largest and the Arctic (represented by the word *article*) being the smallest. The word *ocean* can also help you remember that the mnemonic is about the world's oceans!

The **Pacific Ocean** covers about one-third of the world's surface and holds almost as much water as the other three oceans combined. It stretches from Asia more than 12,000 miles east to the Americas. There are around 25,000 islands in the Pacific Ocean, including New Guinea, the Philippines, Hawaii, New Zealand, and Taiwan.

The **Atlantic Ocean** is the second-largest ocean, covering about one-fifth of the surface of the earth. This *S*-shaped body of water snakes between Latin America and Africa and winds northward between the Americas and Europe. The most notable feature is the Mid-Atlantic Ridge, the underwater mountain range that runs the length of the ocean.

The **Indian Ocean,** the third-largest ocean, covers about 15 percent of the earth's surface. The Indian Ocean is bordered by Antarctica, Africa, southern Asia, and Australia. This body of water has historical importance, first as the site of the earliest known civilizations and later as a major trade route between Asia and Africa.

The **Arctic Ocean,** the smallest ocean, covers only 2 percent of the earth. The basin of the Arctic is a more or less circular area around the North Pole. The chilly climate of the Arctic is characterized by polar icebergs that prevent marine travel for two-thirds of the year.

 *Get This . . .*

Did you know that some people consider the sea surrounding Antarctica to be the world's fifth ocean? This body of water has long been differentiated by mariners as the Southern Ocean because of its distinct currents. In 2000, the International Hydrographic Organization officially recognized the Southern Ocean, although many organizations still disagree with this definition. 🙢

The Countries of Central America

▶ **Mex**i's **gua**camole **be**ats **El**len's **hon**ey 'n' **Cos**ette's **pan**cakes.

Central America is the narrow strip of land that stretches between the Pacific Ocean and the Caribbean Sea, connecting Mexico and the northwest tip of South America. Although the region is technically part of the North American continent, it has a distinctive culture stemming from the rich history of its indigenous peoples.

Each word in the mnemonic stands for a Central American country. For example, *honey* represents Honduras and *pancakes* represents Panama because they share the same beginning letters. The mnemonic not only helps you remember all the countries in Central America, but also lists them in geographical order.

The countries of Central America, roughly from northwest to southeast, are **Mexico, Guatemala, Belize, El Salvador, Honduras, Nicaragua, Costa Rica,** and **Panama.** (Note that only the southeastern-most portion of Mexico is considered part of Central America.)

As you read each word in the mnemonic sentence, put your finger on the corresponding country on the map of Central America above. This will help reinforce the connection between the mnemonic words and the country names.

Memory tools you can count on...

Rational vs. Irrational Numbers

Rational numbers are numbers that can be expressed as a fraction in which the numerator and denominator are integers and the denominator does not equal 0. For example, 0.5 (which can be written as $\frac{1}{2}$), $-\frac{9}{4}$, and 3 (which is the same as $\frac{3}{1}$) are all rational numbers.

Irrational numbers are values that can be written as decimals that never end or repeat. One example of an irrational number is π, which is equal to 3.1415 . . . Some other examples of irrational numbers are $\sqrt{2}$ and 2.6457 . . .

To remember the difference between irrational and rational numbers, try to imagine a crazy person ranting in a never-ending, never-repeating tirade.

. . . .
IT'S YOUR TURN

Write something rational. Be sure it ends with a period. Then, write something irrational. You should be sure to write something that doesn't repeat or end. Be as crazy as you want to be. Just make sure it ends with an ellipsis, the three dots that show a continuation (. . .).

Rational: Ending

Irrational: Never-ending, never-repeating

Division Terms

There are three main terms associated with division. The **dividend** is the number that is being divided by a number, the **divisor** is the number that is being divided into a number, and the quotient is the result. Because *dividend* and *divisor* sound alike, many people confuse the terms.

Here's a good way to remember which term is which.

▶ The divid**end** is on the **end** of a division problem.

Take the problem 120 ÷ 10 = 12, for instance. We know that the quotient—in this case, 12—is usually on the "back end" of the problem, next to the equal sign. The dividend is usually the number on the "front end" of the problem—in this case, 120. That leaves 10 as the divisor, which is in the middle of the problem, between the division sign and the equal sign.

Say your teacher writes the problem $\frac{46}{12}$ = ? on the board and calls on you to identify the dividend. You can still use the memory trick above, but you first have to rewrite the problem using the division sign. Remember that the fraction bar means "divide." So, you can rewrite the problem as 46 ÷ 12 = ?, and you'll see that 46 is on the front end, so it's the dividend. When faced with long division ($12\overline{)46}$), you'll need to rewrite the problem in number sentence form too.

Steps for Long Division

Say you are away at summer camp and you want to buy postcards to send to your friends and family. You have $11 to spend on postcards, which cost $0.65 each. How will you figure out how many postcards you're able to afford with $11? Keep in mind that you don't love your calculator enough to bring it with you to summer camp!

You would probably set up a long division problem in this situation, right? Maybe it has been a while since you learned the process for long division. Can you remember how it's done? One way to remember the steps for long division is to picture the members of the Longdivision family.

▶ The members of Longdivision family are **D**ad, **M**other, **S**ister, **B**rother.

When performing long division, the first step is **divide.** The next step is **multiply.** The third step is **subtract.** The fourth step is **bring down.** (Note that the Longdivisions also have a dog named **R**over and they consider him a member of the family. Depending on the problem, there could be another step that requires you to **repeat** steps 1 through 4 or write the **remainder.**)

Look at the following example of the steps for long division.

Example:

$$5 \overline{)64} \quad \begin{array}{l} \text{DIVIDE: 5 can go into 6 only 1 time.} \\ \text{MULTIPLY: } 1 \times 5 = 5 \\ \text{SUBTRACT: } 6 - 5 = 1 \end{array}$$

$$5 \overline{)64} \quad \text{Bring down the 4.}$$

$$5 \overline{)64} \quad \begin{array}{l} \\ \text{DIVIDE: 5 can go into 14 just 2 times.} \\ \text{MULTIPLY: } 2 \times 5 = 10 \\ \text{SUBTRACT: } 14 - 10 = 4 \end{array}$$
(12 r4)

Parts of a Fraction

▶ The nUmerator is **U**p, the **D**enominator is **D**own.

Fractions represent parts of a whole or parts of a set. For example, if a pie had 8 slices and you ate 3 of those slices, you could use the fraction $\frac{3}{8}$ to describe the portion of the pie that you ate.

The number above the fraction bar is called the **numerator,** and it tells the number of parts being counted. The number below the fraction bar is called the **denominator,** and it tells the total number of equal parts in the whole or in the set.

The word *numerator* has a \u\ sound, which can remind you of the word *up*. The word *denominator* starts with the letter *d*, which can remind you of the word *down*.

To help remember which part of the fraction is the numerator and which is the denominator, you may want to visualize the word *numerator* above the word *denominator*. For example, take a mental snapshot of the following image: $\frac{numerator}{denominator}$.

In order to keep this information straight, you could write each term—*numerator* and *denominator*—on a separate index card. Then, find a horizontal bar, like the towel bar in the bathroom. Tape the word *numerator* to the wall above the bar and tape the word *denominator* to the wall below the bar. This way, you'll have a visual reminder every time you get out of the shower!

Finding the Greatest Common Factor

Sometimes, you will be asked to write a fraction in **simplest form.** This means reducing the fraction so that the numerator and denominator do not share any factors greater than 1. For example, you probably know that $\frac{50}{100}$ reduces to $\frac{1}{2}$. The fractions are equivalent, but $\frac{1}{2}$ is the fraction in simplest form.

One technique for reducing a fraction is finding the greatest common factor of the numerator and the denominator. The **greatest common factor,** or GCF, is the biggest whole number that divides evenly into both numbers. There are three steps you should follow to find the GCF.

▶ The pegword for *one* is *bun.* The picture of the "Grocery LIST" that has only one item, buns, should remind you that the first step in finding the GCF of two numbers is to make a list of all the factors of each number.

The pegword for *two* is *shoe.* The two rows of shoes that show the matching pairs circled and connected should remind you of the second step in finding the GCF. The second step is to circle all the factors that are shared by both numbers.

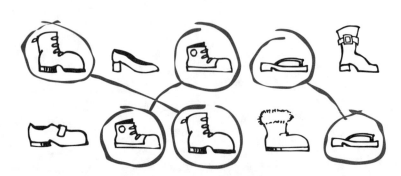

The pegword for *three* is *tree*. The row of trees that shows one tree that is much larger than the rest should remind you of the third step in finding the GCF, which is choosing the greatest number from all the circled factors. This number is the greatest common factor.

Once you've found the GCF, you can divide both the numerator and the denominator by this number in order to write the fraction in simplest form.

Example:

Write the fraction $\frac{45}{60}$ in simplest form.

Step 1: Factors of 45: 1, 3, 5, 9, 15, 45

Factors of 60: 1, 2, 3, 4, 5, 6, 10, 12, 15, 20, 30, 60

Step 2: Factors of 45: ⓵ ③ ⑤ 9, ⑮ 45

Factors of 60: ① 2, ③ 4, ⑤ 6, 10, 12, ⑮ 20, 30, 60

Step 3: Greatest common factor = 15

Now, we can reduce the fraction: $\frac{45}{60} = \frac{45 \div 15}{60 \div 15} = \frac{3}{4}$

So, $\frac{45}{60}$ in simplest form is $\frac{3}{4}$.

Adding and Multiplying Fractions

▶ You can add fractions that have the same bottom;
Then, only the top numbers sum.
You can multiply fractions any old time—
top times top and bottom times bottom.

This rhyme will help you remember the correct way to add and multiply fractions. In the mnemonic, *top* stands for the numerator and *bottom* stands for the denominator. When adding fractions, remember that you can only add fractions that have the same denominator. If the denominators are not equal, you should find the least common denominator. Be sure to add only the numerators when summing two like fractions. The denominators do not change.

Example:

$$\frac{1}{7} + \frac{2}{7} = \frac{1+2}{7} = \frac{3}{7}$$

When multiplying fractions, it doesn't matter whether the denominators are the same, but it is important to remember to multiply the numerators together and to multiply the denominators together.

Example:

$$\frac{2}{5} \times \frac{2}{5} = \frac{2 \times 2}{5 \times 5} = \frac{4}{25}$$

Repeat this rhyme aloud several times. That way, the next time you are presented with a problem where you have to perform operations on fractions, you can repeat this rhyme to yourself!

Prime Numbers

► A **prime** is just divisible by itself and 1.
Like **2** shoes, **3** wishes, or **5** sides of a pentagon.
The **7** Wonders of the World are sure to make you swoon!
Like folks did when *Apollo 11* put man on the moon.
13 is the unlucky prime, so we'll just leave it be.
Let's read ***Seventeen*** magazine or see an "R" movie!

A prime number is a number that has only two factors: itself and 1. Use the rhyming song above to remember the definition of a prime number and the first seven prime numbers: 2, 3, 5, 7, 11, 13, and 17.

Prime numbers have fascinated mathematicians throughout history. Sometimes it is difficult to determine whether or not a number is a prime, especially if it is a big number. Also, did you know that there are infinitely many primes? Some mathematicians devote their entire lives to finding ways to generate prime numbers.

Prime numbers are also important because every nonprime number, or *composite number*, can be broken down into prime factors. For example, the number 36 can be written as $2 \times 2 \times 3 \times 3$. Finding prime factors of numbers is helpful in finding common factors between two numbers.

Complete the following activity, called the Sieve of Eratosthenes. Using a 10-by-10 sheet of graph paper, number the boxes across from 1 to 100. First, cross out the number 1 because it is not prime (a prime number must have *exactly* two factors). Next, move to the number 2. The number 2 is prime, so circle the number 2. Then, cross out all the multiples of 2, such as 4, 6, and 8. These numbers cannot be primes because they have 2 as a factor. Next, move to the number 3 and circle it. Cross out all of the numbers that are multiples of 3. The next number that is not circled or crossed out is 5. Circle the 5 and cross out all the multiples of 5. Continue this process. Whenever you come to a number that is not crossed out, circle it because it's prime. Eventually, you'll be left with all the prime numbers from 1 to 100!

Multiplying by 9

You're probably pretty good with your times tables by now, but it's possible that you get tripped up occasionally. Many people struggle with their 9 facts. Maybe you've heard the rule about the sum of the digits of the product adding up to 9 when you multiply by 9 (for example, $7 \times 9 = 63$ and $6 + 3 = 9$). Here is another pretty cool trick that can help you multiply by 9.

▶ Turn both of your hands palms up. Say you want to multiply 9 by 5. Start with the finger farthest to the left (the thumb of your left hand). Now count in 5 fingers and bend down the fifth finger (it should be your left pinky). The number of fingers to the left of the finger that's bent down is the first digit of the product (4) and the number of fingers to the right of the finger that's bent down is the second digit of the product (5).

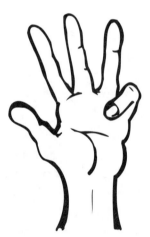 

. . . .
It's Your Turn

Now, try multiplying 9 by any other one-digit number and see if the trick works. Teach your new trick to a friend or family member and make sure you can explain it well—being able to explain a concept is a great sign that you've mastered it.

Absolute Value

I am a changed number, with a positive outlook!

The **absolute value** of a number is the distance from zero to that number on the number line. Thus, the absolute value of a positive number is simply the number itself. The absolute value of a negative number is the opposite of that number. For example, the absolute value of –1, written as $|-1|$ is equal to 1, because –1 is 1 unit from zero on the number line.

Do you believe that bad numbers can be reformed? Use the mnemonic to help you remember that the absolute value of a negative number always yields the opposite, positive value. The absolute value bars resemble a jail, so think of the "prison time" as transforming the negative numbers into positive numbers! (If only it were that easy with hardened criminals, right?)

. . . .
It's Your Turn

The graph of the absolute value function resembles a "V" shape. When the input value is positive, the output is just the same number. This creates the right side of the "V." When the input is negative, the output is opposite of the input value. This creates the left side of the "V." Come up with your own mnemonic for remembering what the graph of the absolute value function looks like. Experiment using the different types of mnemonics that you have learned so far in this book!

Adding Positive and Negative Numbers

▶ GADS

Adding positive and negative numbers can be tricky! GADS is an acronym for the rule for determining the sign of the sum of a positive number and a negative number. It stands for **"G**reater **A**bsolute value **D**ecides **S**ign." (Remember that the absolute value of a number is the distance from zero to that number on the number line.)

When you are adding two numbers with opposite signs, find the difference of their absolute values. Using GADS, the sum should get the sign of the number with the greater absolute.

For example, suppose we want to find the sum of –7 and 5. First, we should take the absolute value of both of these integers. The absolute value of –7 is 7 and the absolute value of 5 is 5. That means that our final sum will be negative, because –7 has a greater absolute value than 5. Next, we should find the difference between 7 and 5. We know that 7 – 5 = 2. Therefore, our final answer is –2.

❝ Get This . . .

Have you ever heard of an abacus? Long before calculators were invented, the Chinese came up with a method for adding very large numbers by sliding beads back and forth along strings. Today, many students in China still learn to use an abacus to find the sums and differences of very large numbers without even needing pencil and paper. Some students practice addition with the abacus so often that eventually they can find the sums without even using the abacus! They have a sort of "finger memory" that allows them to mimic the movement of the abacus by waving their fingers through the air, sliding imaginary beads back and forth. **❞**

Multiplying Positive and Negative Numbers

▶ If the signs match, that's a plus (+).
  If the signs clash, that's a bust (–).

This rhyme will help you remember the correct sign to use when multiplying positive and negative numbers. The product of two positive numbers will always be positive. Also, the product of two negative numbers will always be negative. In other words, if the two factors have the same sign—or if the signs "match"—then the product is always positive.

Examples:

$6 \times 7 = 42$

$-6 \times -7 = 42$

Any time you multiply a positive number by a negative number, the product will be negative. In other words, if the two factors have different signs—or if their signs "clash"—then the product is always negative.

Examples:

$-4 \times 5 = -20$

$7 \times -9 = -63$

· · · · · · · · · · · ·
IT'S YOUR TURN

What do you think would happen if you multiplied three numbers with varying signs (for example, two positive numbers and a negative number, or three negative numbers)? Use the associative property (see pages 160–161) and the rhyme above to help you come up with a rule for multiplying more than two numbers with varying signs. Once you come up with a rule, create a rhyme to help you remember it!

The Order of Operations

▶ **P**lease **E**xcuse **M**y **D**ear **A**unt **S**ally.

The **order of operations** is the sequence in which you should perform operations to simplify algebraic expressions. The mnemonic above will help you remember the order in which to perform each operation. The first letter of each word in the acrostic stands for a mathematical symbol or operation.

The P stands for **parentheses.** You should always complete operations inside parentheses first. The E stands for **exponents.** Exponential expressions should be simplified next. The M and D stand for **multiplication** and **division.** You should perform these operations in the order that they appear, from left to right. Finally, the A and S stand for **addition** and **subtraction.** Again, perform these operations in the order that they appear from left to right.

Example:

Let's use the order of operations to simplify $3 + 2^2 \times 7 - (9 - 8) \div 0.5$.

Parentheses: $3 + 2^2 \times 7 - \mathbf{(9 - 8)} \div 0.5 = 3 + 2^2 \times 7 - \mathbf{1} \div 0.5$
Exponents: $3 + \mathbf{2^2} \times 7 - 1 \div 0.5 = 3 + \mathbf{4} \times 7 - 1 \div 0.5$
Multiplication/Division (from left to right): $3 + \mathbf{4 \times 7} - \mathbf{1 \div 0.5} =$
$$3 + \mathbf{28} - \mathbf{2}$$
Addition/Subtraction (from left to right): $\mathbf{3 + 28 - 2 = 29}$

Imagine your hypothetical Aunt Sally doing something rude that she should be excused for. Did she forget your best friend's name? Did she talk with food in her mouth? Maybe she did something very inappropriate. Invent an image for your Aunt Sally and decide what awful thing she did. You can even draw this image in the margin of your math homework to help you remember the order of operations, as long as it's not too inappropriate.

The Digits of Pi

▶ May I have a large milkshake, no cherry added?

The number **pi,** or π, is very important in mathematics. You may have used the number pi when calculating the circumference or the area of a circle. Pi is a nonrepeating, nonterminating decimal. That means that the digits in pi do not repeat and that the decimal goes on forever without ending. Numbers like this are called "irrational numbers." Can you figure out how the mnemonic above can be used to remember the first nine digits of pi: 3.14159265?

Notice that the number of letters in each word corresponds to a successive digit in pi. For example, the first word (*May*) has 3 letters, the second word (*I*) has 1 letter, the third word (*have*) has 4 letters, and so on (3.14...).

Here are the first 20 digits of pi: 3.1415926535897932384. Try to come up with a poem using the number of letters in each word to represent successive digits as in the mnemonic above. To make it easier to remember the poem, write about a topic that is particularly interesting to you, such as one of your favorite hobbies.

66 *Get This . . .*

Some mathematicians devote much of their lives to exploring the number pi and to developing different ways to memorize the digits of pi. Many different mnemonics have been used, including the method mentioned above. Another method that is used is "chunking" the digits. You may memorize your phone number by chunking the area code, the first three digits, and the last four digits. A similar method can be used for memorizing the digits of pi. Pi enthusiasts chunk three or four digits at a time and then recite the digits over and over until they have memorized them. The current world record for memorizing digits of pi belongs to Hiroyuki Goto of Japan. He has memorized and recited the first 42,195 digits! 99

Properties of Numbers

► **A**my text-messaged **B**arbara to tell her that, on the **commute** home, she saw their friend flirting with some dorky sixth grader on the bus. **B**arbara text-messaged **A**my back to say she had seen the same thing.

Ten minutes later, **A**my called **B**arbara, who was on the other line with **C**handra, telling her that Amy was spreading nasty rumors about her. **B**arbara called **A**my back, and a few minutes later, **C**handra on the other line to ask Barbara why she would **associate** with a nasty rumor-spreader.

Amy decided to nip this in the bud. She called each of her friends individually. **A**my to **B**arbara: "You're a traitor." **A**my to **C**handra: "You're a flirt." But neither of them particularly cared what Amy thought. Who was she to **distribute** insults when she was the queen of all gossips?

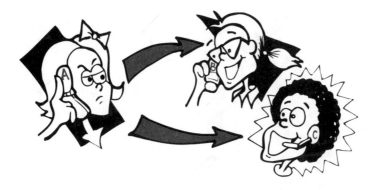

The commutative, associative, and distributive properties are important rules to know when adding and multiplying. The highlighted words in the story above will help you remember the meanings of each of these properties. As you read the story, think about how the girls' interactions reflect each property.

Here are definitions of the properties. Let a, b, and c be real numbers.

Commutative Property: $a + b = b + a$

$$a \cdot b = b \cdot a$$

Associative Property: $a + (b + c) = (a + b) + c$

$$a \cdot (b \cdot c) = (a \cdot b) \cdot c$$

Distributive Property: $a \cdot (b + c) = a \cdot b + a \cdot c$

Can you see how the story about Amy, Barbara, and Chandra mirrors each of these properties?

Use blocks or any other household item, like toothpicks or pennies, to help you visualize the properties above. For example, start with one pile of 2 blocks, and one pile of 3 blocks. To demonstrate the commutative property, start by adding the pile of 2 blocks to the pile of 3 blocks. Prove to yourself that the sum is the same when you physically switch the order of the two piles. Model the associative and distributive properties too. Once you have practiced these properties on something physical, you can picture the process when you are working with numbers!

Dividing by Zero

▶ Never sit on a beach ball!

In mathematics, dividing a real number by zero is not allowed! We say that the quotient is undefined, or it does not exist.

To understand why this is true, think about dividing the number 10 by 5. The quotient is 2. We also know that if we multiply 5 by 2, the product is 10. This is because multiplication and division are inverse operations. So, if you divide a number, let's say 12, by 0 and you get a real number as the quotient—let's call the real number x—then when you multiply 0 by x, you should get 12. This will never work! Multiplying zero by any number always results in a product of 0.

Use the mnemonic above to help you remember that you can never divide by zero. The beach ball represents zero, and sitting on top of it represents dividing a number by zero. If you sit on a beach ball, it will pop!

It's Your Turn

The number zero has many special properties. It is the additive identity. This means, if you add zero to any number, you get the original number as the sum. Furthermore, zero multiplied by any number is always zero, and zero divided by any nonzero number is always zero. Try to come up with clever phrases such as the one above to help you remember these other special properties of the number zero.

Scientific Notation

► **Positive power**, move in the **positive** direction.
Negative power, move in the **negative** direction.

Scientific notation is an abbreviated way of writing very large or very small numbers. As the mnemonic above suggests, when a number is written in scientific notation and you want to write its value in standard notation, you move the decimal point either to the right or to the left, depending on whether the exponent is positive or negative. You move the decimal point the number of spaces indicated by the exponent.

Remember that the *positive* direction means "to the right." Think of moving in the direction of the positive numbers on the number line. The *negative* direction means "to the left." Think of moving in the direction of the negative numbers on the number line.

Let's write 5×10^6 in standard notation. Remember, 5 can be written as 5.0000 . . . , with any number of zeros after the decimal point.

Because the power is positive and equal to six, that means you should move the decimal point 6 places to the right, in the *positive* direction.

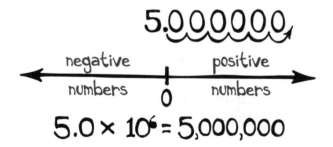

When you are counting the number of spaces the decimal point moves, bounce your pointer finger under the numbers as if it is following the path of a bouncing "ball" (the decimal point). Each time you bounce one space, count it off. This will help ensure that you move the decimal point the correct number of places.

Negative Exponents

► The exhausted swimmer had **negative power** going into the last **flip-turn**.

Have you ever done a flip-turn in the swimming pool? Competitive swimmers use this technique when they get to the end of the pool in order to change direction quickly. Use this mnemonic to help you remember how to simplify an expression with a **negative power,** or exponent.

Let's say we have x^{-2}. We know that's the same as $\frac{x^{-2}}{1}$. The phrase "flip-turn" will help you remember that the first step is to *flip* the fraction to $\frac{1}{x^{-2}}$, and the next step is to *turn* the sign from negative to positive: $\frac{1}{x^2}$. So, we know that $x^{-2} = \frac{1}{x^2}$.

We can simplify exponential expressions when the base is a number too.

Example:

$$2^{-3} = \frac{2^{-3}}{1}$$

Flip the fraction: $\frac{1}{2^{-3}}$

Turn the sign: $\frac{1}{2^3}$

Simplify: $\frac{1}{2^3} = \frac{1}{2 \times 2 \times 2} = \frac{1}{8}$

Flipping and turning are probably motions that you are familiar with. As you are memorizing the mnemonic and simplifying exponential expressions, come up with a hand motion to mimic the motion of flipping and turning. In fact, you may want your hand motion for flip to show movement from the top to the bottom, mimicking the motion of moving between the numerator and the denominator. For turn you could spin your finger around or come up with another motion that reminds you to change the sign of the exponent.

Raising a Base to the Zero Power

▶ If you look into the sun,
you get one!

Raising any nonzero number to the power of zero yields one. If you know how to manipulate exponential expressions, you will understand why.

Imagine you have $\dfrac{x^5}{x^3}$. To divide two powers with the same base, simply subtract the exponents. So, $\dfrac{x^5}{x^3} = x^{5-3} = x^2$. Now, imagine if the exponential expression in the numerator were equal to the expression in the denominator, for example, in $\dfrac{x^2}{x^2}$. Just looking at this expression, we know that any number divided by itself equals 1. If we simplify this expression according to the properties of exponents, then $\dfrac{x^2}{x^2} = x^{2-2} = x^0$. This proves that $x^0 = 1$.

Use the rhyming mnemonic to help you remember that raising a number to the zero power equals 1. Looking into the sun represents a number being raised to the zero power, since the round shape of the sun resembles the shape of a zero. The result of raising a number to the zero power will *always* be one. (Zero raised to the power of zero is not one, however. This value is called an *indeterminate*.)

Next time you come across a problem in math class that requires you to take a number to the zero power, look up at the ceiling light as you recite the rhyming mnemonic. (Don't actually look out the window at the sun because this could damage your vision or give you one serious headache!) This action will reinforce the rhyme, helping you remember that any nonzero number to the zero power is 1.

Proportions

▶ "apPROpriate PORTIONS"

You probably know that a ratio is a comparison of two values. If a class has 20 girls and 10 boys, then the ratio of girls to boys is 20:10, which can be reduced to 2:1. That means that for every 2 girls in the class, there is 1 boy. Let's say that another class in the same school has 16 girls and 8 boys. The ratio of girls to boys in this class is 16:8, which can be reduced to 2:1. Notice that the ratios are the same. In each class, there are 2 girls for every 1 boy. That means these two classes have *proportionate* numbers of girls and boys. In a **proportion,** two ratios are equal.

The picture on the previous page illustrates the keywords *appropriate portions* because each person is eating the right amount for his size. The big body builder is about to eat a huge portion of pizza. The small kid is going to eat only one slice. That means that each person's serving size is *proportionate* to his body size.

Imagine the body builder weighs 280 pounds and is eating 7 slices of pizza. The ratio of his weight to his portion of pizza is 280:7, which can be reduced to 40:1. Now, let's say the kid weighs just 40 pounds and has only 1 slice of pizza. This represents the same ratio, 40:1. The body builder is several times bigger than the tiny kid, so he is eating several times more pizza!

If you're having trouble remembering what *proportion* means, try to remember this picture.

Roman Numerals

The number system that you use in math class is called the Arabic system. Arabic numerals use only ten different symbols: the digits 0 through 9. This system relies on the concept of place value, with each place representing ten times the value of the next place to the right. The Arabic number system is very efficient, but it is not the only number system that we use.

You probably see **Roman numerals** all the time, in the titles of movies (*Rocky V*), in outlines for school reports (II. The Properties of Waves), and in the names of sporting events (Superbowl XL). But do you know what each Roman numeral stands for? You can use the following mnemonic to remember the seven symbols, in order from the least value (1) to the greatest value (1,000).

▶ **In Vince's "X-treme" Lullaby, Cows Destroy Men.**

I = 1
V = 5
X = 10
L = 50
C = 100
D = 500
M = 1,000

So, the year 1708 would be written as MDCCVIII. Can you see why we would choose to use the Arabic number system over Roman numerals?

Imagine a guy named Vince who can't fall asleep, so he listens to a lullaby about counting sheep. But then, in the same field in which he's picturing the sheep, he imagines some evil cows grazing. And then those homicidal cows suddenly turn on the poor shepherds. Not a very pleasant bedtime story, is it? But if you can make up a sweet-sounding lullaby to go along with this gory story, we bet you'll never forget the mnemonic!

. . . .
IT'S YOUR TURN

Now, it's your turn to try using Roman numerals. If you wanted to write 1,254, it would look like this: MCCLIV. The M stands for 1,000, CC stands for 200, the L stands for 50, and IV stands for 4. (Although you might think that 4 should be written as IIII, in Roman numerals, you place a smaller numeral in front of a larger numeral to indicate subtraction.) Practice writing the following numbers using Roman numerals.

1. 34   3. 3,164
2. 226   4. 573

Multiplying Binomials

▶ The FOIL method

A **binomial** is a polynomial with two terms. When you are multiplying two binomials such as $(x + 2)$ and $(x + 3)$, it is important that each term in the first binomial is multiplied by each term in the second binomial. To do this in a systematic way, use the FOIL method.

$(x + 2)(x + 3)$

First: Multiply together the "first" terms in each binomial. $x \cdot x = x^2$

Outside: Multiply the first term of the first binomial by the second term in the second binomial. $x \cdot 3 = 3x$

Inside: Multiply the second term of the first binomial by the first term of the second binomial. $2 \cdot x = 2x$

Last: Multiply together the "last" terms in each binomial. $2 \cdot 3 = 6$

After you have multiplied the terms, be sure to simplify and combine like terms. $x^2 + 2x + 3x + 6 = x^2 + 5x + 6$

You may find it useful to draw a line to connect the terms that are supposed to be multiplied. As you connect the first terms in each binomial, write the word first above the line. Continue this until you have connected the outside, inside, and last terms. By connecting the terms of the binomials, you can check that each term in the first binomial is indeed multiplied by each term in the second binomial.

Domain and Range

▶ Doma**IN** goes **IN**, range comes out.

Some students confuse domain and range. The **domain** of a function is the set of all x-values that can go *into* the function. The **range** is the set of all corresponding y-values that come *out* of the function.

For example, imagine you were having a pizza sale as a fund-raiser for school. Each student was allowed to sell up to 20 pizzas for $6 each. You came up with an equation to show how much money students could collect by selling different numbers of pizzas. The domain, or x-values, could represent the number of pizzas sold and the range, or y-values, could represent the amount of money collected. In this situation, the domain is restricted. You cannot have domain values less than 0, because that would represent selling negative pizzas, and the maximum domain value is 20, because each student may only sell up to 20 pizzas.

In school, you may have seen functions represented by "function machines." This is an appropriate model for a function, because x-values go into a function, a particular operation is performed on them, and then y-values come out. In the picture below, notice how the x-values are coming from a box of domain values. They go into the "function machine," and y-values come out, to be deposited into the box marked *range*. When you are working with domain and range, try to visualize this picture.

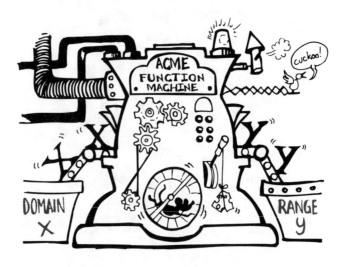

The Coordinate Plane

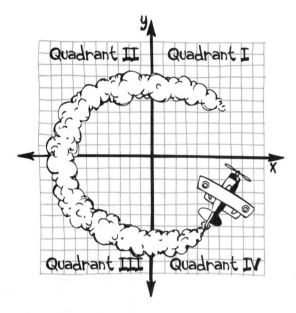

▶ The Coordinate "Plane" writes a "C."

A coordinate plane is the two-dimensional plane that contains the x- and y-axes. The axes divide the coordinate plane into four regions. Each region is called a **quadrant** (*quad* means four).

In the mnemonic above, the plane spins up and around. It passes through the first quadrant, then the second, and finally the third and the fourth. You can tell because the plane is doing skywriting and has outlined the letter C. The quadrants are often numbered with Roman numerals, so you can think of the top-right section where the plane starts as Quadrant I, the top-left section as Quadrant II, and so on. If you ever have trouble remembering how the quadrants are numbered, just draw a C on the coordinate plane.

👁 You could use mnemonics to help you remember other characteristics of the coordinate plane. One idea might be to label the airplane in the picture *BYNX*. As you go around the quadrants, the letters will help you remember which of the values are positive. For example, in quadrant one **b**oth x and y are positive. In quadrant two, **y** is positive. In quadrant three, **n**either is positive, and in quadrant four, **x** is positive.

Plotting a Coordinate Pair

It's a common error to confuse the order of the *x*- and *y*-coordinates in a coordinate pair. To help remember which coordinate comes first, just remember the following rhyme.

▶ *x* before **y**, **walk** before you **fly**.

Look at the coordinate grid below. Check out the guy walking across the *x*-axis, then flying up alongside the *y*-axis.

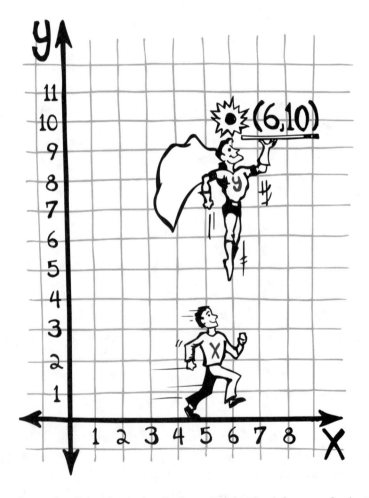

The guy walking horizontally is at (6, 0). That's because he is 6 spaces to the right of the origin, so he is on 6 on the *x*-axis. And he's 0 points up or down.

The guy flying vertically is at (6, 10). That's because he is 10 spaces above the origin. And he's 6 spaces to the right of the origin.

So, all you have to do is realize that the first number in the coordinate pair tells you how far to *walk* (move horizontally). In this case, that is 6 points to the right of the origin. Then, you get to *fly* (move vertically)! Here, that's all the way up 10 points to (6, 10).

You can remember this mnemonic any time you have to locate the placement of an ordered pair on a coordinate grid. Ask yourself how far (and in which direction) you have to walk. Then, ask yourself how far (and in which direction) you have to fly.

Say the alphabet out loud. When you get to the end, slow down and pronounce *x* and *y* carefully. Do you notice how *x* comes before *y*? Exactly!

Intercepts

▶ "y-intersect"

In the graph of a line, the **y-intercept** is where the line crosses the y-axis and the **x-intercept** is where the line crosses the x-axis. You can remember that the intercepts are the points where the line crosses the axes using the keyword **intersect,** which sounds like *intercept.* You know that *intersect* means to cross through—think about the intersection of two streets; the intercept is where the line meets and crosses through the axis. When you want to figure out the y-intercept, imagine the y-axis is one street and the graphed line is a second street. The point at which the two streets cross, or intersect, is the y-intercept. You can even think of the point that marks the intercept as a red light in the intersection!

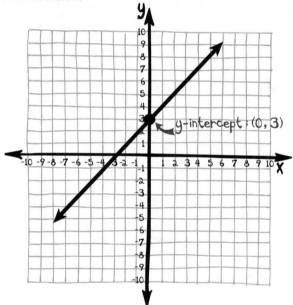

On a large sheet of construction paper, draw a coordinate grid. Then, use markers to add details to the x- and y-axes to make them look like two-lane roads. Next, draw a line that passes through the points (1, 4), (2, 3), and (3, 2). Shade this line thickly in black and use chalk to add white lane-divider lines. Pretend your pencil is a car, and "travel" up the line until you get to the intersection at the y-axis. Then, use your pencil to make a dark dot at this "intersection." What are the coordinates of this y-intercept?

Slope-Intercept Form of a Line

► That **line** over **y**onder is the **M**exican **b**order.

The **slope-intercept form** for the equation of a line is $y = mx + b$, where m represents the slope of a line, and b represents the y-intercept, or the point at which the line crosses the y-axis. For example, in the equation $y = \frac{1}{2}x + 6$, the slope of the line is $\frac{1}{2}$ and the y-intercept is the point (0, 6).

In the mnemonic above, *That line* will help you remember that you are writing the equation of a line. The word *yonder* represents the y in the slope-intercept form of the equation. Next, remember that phrase *is the* indicates where the equal sign belongs. The word *Mexican* should remind you of *mx*; and because the m and the x are represented in one word, remember that they should be right next to each other, indicating multiplication. Finally, the b in *border* should help you remember the b in the slope-intercept form of an equation. Because *border* is a separate word, remember that the b should be added, not multiplied.

The state of Texas borders on Mexico. Pretend you are a Texas rancher leaning up against a fence on your property. Your new neighbor comes by to say hello and you tell him all about the history of the land. At some point in the conversation, be sure to gesture as if you're pointing off into the distance and recite the mnemonic sentence using an exaggerated Texas accent.

Graphing Inequalities

In the United States, people cannot vote until they're 18 years old. If you wanted to write an inequality showing the ages of people who can legally vote, you would write $a \geq 18$. That means that a can be any value that is 18 or above. You can graph this inequality too. Because the value 18 is included (18-year-olds are allowed to vote), you would need to start with a closed, or shaded, point at 18. Then, you would need an arrow facing right to show all the ages over 18.

When you are graphing an inequality, it's easy to confuse when to use a closed dot and when to use an open dot. Because a closed dot means the point is included, you use a closed dot when the inequality has a greater-than-or-equal-to symbol or a less-than-or-equal-to symbol. You use an open dot when the inequality has a greater-than or less-than symbol.

The picture above can help you remember when to use a closed dot and when to use an open dot. The graph shows $x > 3$. The point 3 is not included in the graph of $x > 3$, so the open dot is saying he feels *empty inside* when he's *not included*.

Parallel vs. Perpendicular

Parallel lines are lines in a plane that never intersect. **Perpendicular** lines are lines that intersect to form a right (90-degree) angle. To remember which is which, notice the parallel lines in the word *parallel*.

Remember that a right angle is often indicated by a small square in the corner of the angle. The letter *E* has 4 perpendicular lines, making 4 right angles. So, you might also remember that the *E*s in the word *perpendicular* have many perpendicular lines.

Draw two vertical parallel lines on a sheet of graph paper. Then, write the letters *P-A-R-A* to the left of your lines. Then, write the letters *E-L* to the right of your lines. Do you see what you've written?

Right Angle

▶ The *right* way to sit is with your back straight in the chair.

A **right angle** is formed by two perpendicular lines—in other words, two lines that meet at a 90-degree angle. For example, the back and the seat of a chair meet at a right angle. Imagining a person sitting up straight—the "right" way—in a chair will help you remember the definition of a right angle.

Draw a picture for this mnemonic. You might want to draw a child sitting straight up in his chair, with his mom reminding him that it is the right way to sit, or you could make a "classroom rule" sign about sitting up straight that a teacher might post on a bulletin board (be sure to include a diagram).

The Hypotenuse of a Right Triangle

The **hypotenuse** is the longest side of any right triangle. The other two sides are the legs. The hypotenuse is the side directly across from the right angle. (It almost looks like the right angle "points" to the hypotenuse.) No matter what the measures of the legs are, the hypotenuse will always be the longest side.

Look at the triangle below. What do you notice about the sides and their respective names?

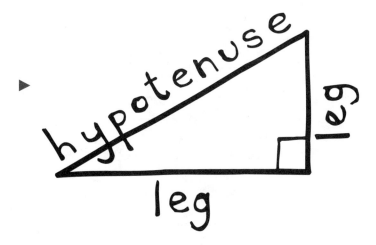

The word *leg* is really short. The word *hypotenuse* is really long. By looking at the names of each side, you can practically tell which side will be the longest! Just remember that *hypotenuse* is a long word to spell, and it's also the longest side of a right triangle.

Say the words *leg, leg* really quickly—as quickly as you can. Say the word *hy-pot-e-nuse* really slowly, drawing out each syllable. This will help you recall that the hypotenuse is the longest part of a right triangle and that the legs are the shorter sides.

The Pythagorean Theorem

► I saw a square hippo with two square legs!

Right triangles have many unique properties. The **Pythagorean theorem** states that the square of the length of the hypotenuse is equal to the sum of the squares of the lengths of the other two sides. The formula is $c^2 = a^2 + b^2$, where c equals the length of the hypotenuse.

The *square hippo* in this mnemonic will help you remember to square the hypotenuse (c^2). The word *with* joins the two parts of the sentence, so this word can help you remember that there should be an equal sign. The *two square legs* mean that you should square the length of each leg of the triangle and then add them together ($a^2 + b^2$). When you think of the Pythagorean theorem, you can think of this silly picture of a square hippo with two square legs.

Here is an example of the Pythagorean theorem.

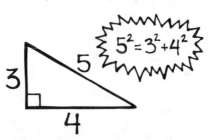

Types of Angles

No matter how advanced you are in math, you'll need to remember the three basic types of angles: acute, right, and obtuse.

An **acute** angle has a measure of less than 90 degrees. Use the picture below to help you remember that *acute* triangles refer to triangles with angles less than 90 degrees. An angle less than 90 degrees is called an *acute* angle. *Acute* sounds like *cute,* which should help you think of smaller angles (because small things are often considered cute).

An **obtuse** angle has a measure of more than 90 degrees. *Obtuse* sounds like *obese,* which should help you think of bigger angles.

▶ A **cute** puppy is a small dog. An **acute** angle is a small angle.
An **obese** dog is a very large dog. An **obtuse** angle is a large angle.

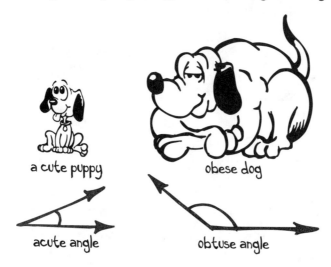

a cute puppy   obese dog

acute angle   obtuse angle

And of course, a **right** angle has a measure of exactly 90 degrees. (For more information about right angles, see page 178.)

As you think about acute, obtuse, and right angles, create an example angle with your arms. Remember that a right angle looks like a straight-backed chair. You can stick one arm straight out and one arm straight up. To create an acute angle, lower your top arm toward the arm that is extended out so that they are almost touching. For an obtuse angle, extend your top arm back past your head. This will not only help you remember an obtuse angle, but also help you stretch!

Scalene, Isosceles, and Equilateral Triangles

There are many ways to classify triangles. One way is to count the number of congruent, or equal, sides.

- A triangle with three congruent sides is called **equilateral.**
- A triangle with at least two congruent sides is called **isosceles.**
- A triangle with no congruent sides is **scalene.**

▶ To remember what each word means, look at the first letter of each term: E, I, and S.

- There are 3 congruent, horizontal lines in the **E**. That is the number of congruent sides in an **equilateral** triangle.
- There are 2 congruent, horizontal lines in the **I**. That is the minimum number of congruent sides in an **isosceles** triangle.
- There are no congruent, horizontal lines in the **S**. That is the number of congruent sides in a **scalene** triangle.

Draw your own equilateral, isosceles, and scalene triangles. Use a ruler to make sure you draw 3, 2, and no congruent sides, respectively, for the three triangles.

Perimeter vs. Area

► pe-RIM-e-ter

Sometimes students confuse area and perimeter. **Area** is a measure of the amount of two-dimensional space an object covers. For example, if you buy a rug that is 8 feet by 10 feet, it will cover a floor area of 80 square feet.

Perimeter, on the other hand, is a measure of the distance around an object. For example, that same rug that measures 8 feet by 10 feet would have a perimeter of 36 feet. To find the perimeter of a rectangle, you just have to add the lengths of all four sides. In this case, the perimeter would be 8 feet + 8 feet + 10 feet + 10 feet = 36 feet.

A good way to remember that perimeter is the distance around an object is to emphasize the second syllable of the word, as in pe-RIM-e-ter. You probably know that a rim is the outer edge of a surface. So, if you wanted to measure the perimeter of a plate, you would find the length around the rim, or border, of the plate.

Say the word *perimeter* out loud, but pronounce the syllable *rim* much louder than the rest of the word and draw it out dramatically, as if you're reciting a sacred chant. While you're chanting, you can even use your pencil to play a drum beat on the *rim* (or outer edge) of your desk. Just be sure not to do this while the teacher is talking!

Area and Circumference of a Circle

▶ For a circle:
Apple pies are square.
Cherry pies are too!

Most apple pies aren't really square, but maybe a circle would feel strange about eating pies that were shaped like himself! This chaining mnemonic will help you remember the formulas for the area and the circumference of a circle.

The **area** of a circle is the amount of space inside the circle. The second line of the mnemonic represents the formula for the area of a circle: $A = \pi r^2$. *Apple* stands for A, or area; *pies* stands for the number π, and *are square* represents r^2, the radius of the circle being squared.

The **circumference** of a circle is the distance around the circle. The third line of the mnemonic represents the formula for the circumference of a circle: $C = 2\pi r$. *Cherry* stands for C, or circumference. Again, *pies* stand for the number π. Finally, *are too* represents r, the radius, times 2. Notice that the order of the multiplication is different. Our mnemonic actually stands for $C = \pi r \cdot 2$. But remember, multiplication is commutative, so the order doesn't matter!

Be careful! It is important to remember which formula applies to which type of pie. If you simply memorize the picture, it may be difficult to remember how the picture relates to the formulas. So, use the picture, but also say the mnemonic over and over in your head until you've memorized it.

Quadrilaterals

▶ Poor **Rhombus** the rhinoceros was in a car **rectangle** while trying to avoid a **square**-ell, and he ended up **trapezoid** in a **parallelogram** universe.

A **quadrilateral** is any polygon with four sides. This mnemonic will help you remember the five main types of quadrilaterals.

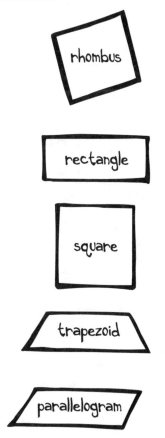

A **rhombus** is a quadrilateral with opposite sides that are parallel and four congruent sides. Rhombus is the name of the unfortunate rhinoceros who is the driver in this story.

A **rectangle** is a quadrilateral with four right angles. In the story, the phrase *car rectangle* sounds like *car wreck*.

A **square** is a quadrilateral with four right angles and four congruent sides. The made-up word *square-ell* sounds like *squirrel*.

A **trapezoid** is a quadrilateral with one pair of parallel sides. The word *trapezoid* sounds like *trapped*.

Finally, a **parallelogram** is a quadrilateral in which opposite sides are parallel and congruent. A *parallelogram universe* sounds like a parallel universe.

You may notice that a square is a specific example of a rectangle, and a rhombus is a specific example of a parallelogram. When you are remembering the characteristics of each type of quadrilateral, it is helpful to think about how they relate to each other.

Walk around your house and identify different types of quadrilaterals. Each time you come across a four-sided polygon, think back to the mnemonic and decide which type of quadrilateral you have found.

Metric Prefixes

▶ **Kids have dreams [based on] doing cool math.**

The acrostic above is a way to help you remember the **prefixes of the metric system,** from largest to smallest. The letters in the acrostic stand for **kilo, hecto, deka,** [base], **deci, centi,** and **milli.** Notice that the word *base* is not actually a prefix, but rather a way of representing the base unit (for example, a meter or a gram). The metric system is often the preferred system of measurement because it uses a base ten, which means that all the values in the metric system differ from each other by a power of ten. Take a look at the table below.

Metric Prefixes

Prefix	Power of 10	Number of Meters
kilo	10^3	1000
hecto	10^2	100
deka	10^1	10
base	10^0	1
deci	10^{-1}	0.1
centi	10^{-2}	0.01
milli	10^{-3}	0.001

The chart above shows that 1 kilometer equals 1,000 meters. One centimeter equals 0.01 meters, or one-hundredth of a meter. This also means that 100 centimeters equal a meter.

When trying to remember the prefixes from the acronym above, remember that all the smaller prefixes, such as *deci, centi,* and *milli,* end in the letter *i.* You are probably most familiar with the prefixes *kilo, centi,* and *milli,* but some of the others may sound strange to you at first. Say the prefixes over and over again, in order, so that you can remember the words. Once you have learned the mnemonic and the prefixes, you will be able to remember their order and their meaning.

Converting Measures

If you are grocery shopping or baking, it is important to be able to convert between cups, pints, quarts, and gallons.

It may help to remember the correct size order of cups, pints, quarts, and gallons. One helpful way is to recognize that the lengths of the words correspond to the sizes of the measures.

▶ A **cup** is the smallest unit and it has **3 letters**.
A **pint** is the next biggest unit and it has **4 letters**.
A **quart** is the next biggest unit and it has **5 letters**.
A **gallon** is the largest unit and it has **6 letters**.

It is important to have a sense of the relative sizes of these measures too. To get a sense of the size of the smallest unit, one **cup**, imagine a serving of mashed potatoes or your balled-up fist.

There are 2 cups in a **pint.** If you have ever bought a small container of ice cream at a convenience store and eaten the entire thing, only to find that it is supposed to be four servings, you probably know how much a pint is!

There are 2 pints in a **quart.** If you were buying ice cream for a birthday party, you would probably buy a quart-sized carton.

There are 4 quarts in a **gallon.** A large plastic container of milk can help you remember the size of a gallon.

Open up the refrigerator and freezer and see how many examples of cup-, pint-, quart- and gallon-sized containers you can find. Try to identify the size by sight. You can check your estimates by reading the serving suggestions. If one serving is a half-cup and the container holds 8 servings, you know that the container is quart-sized.

The Distance Formula

▶ "Dirt"

Many math and physics problems require you to know the relationship between distance, rate, and time. The distance formula states that distance equals rate times time, or $d = rt$.

Example:

Imagine that a car was traveling at a rate of 50 miles per hour for 4 hours. You could determine the total distance the car had traveled using the distance formula.

$d = rt$

$d = 50 \dfrac{\text{miles}}{\text{hour}} \times 4 \text{ hours}$

$d = 200 \text{ miles}$

Therefore, the car traveled a distance of 200 miles.

To help you remember the distance formula, remember the keyword *dirt*. This is how the formula **di**stance = **r**ate × **t**ime might sound if you were to abbreviate each term and make a word from the abbreviations.

To help you remember what the *d, r,* and *t* stand for, imagine cars drag racing on a *dirt* road. That way, you can make the connection between the word *dirt* and the equation involving distance, rate, and time. When cars are racing, they travel the same *distance.* They want to have the fastest *rate,* so that they will finish in the shortest amount of *time.*

Scale Drawing

When you look at a map of the United States, the distance from Phoenix to New York City on the map isn't the *actual* distance between those two cities, of course. That would be a pretty big map! But, if the real distance from Phoenix to New York is about twice the distance from Kansas City to New York, then the distance from Phoenix to New York on the map is about twice the distance from Kansas City to New York on the map. This is because a map is a type of **scale drawing.** A map is a scaled-down version of reality. Maybe 1 inch on the map equals 200 miles. So, the scale of the map is the ratio 1 inch : 200 miles.

In the picture above, the artist is using his thumb to create a scale drawing of the scale! If the scale is 12 inches high in reality and 6 inches high in the painting, then the scale of the painting is 1:2. Each inch in the painting represents 2 inches in real life. So, if the apple next to the scale is actually 3 inches tall, then it should be 1.5 inches high in the painting. That way, the apple looks the right size compared to the scale. Remembering this picture can help you remember the meaning of a scale drawing, or in this case, painting!

Measures of Central Tendency

▶ *Mode* sounds like *most*.
Median sounds like *medium*.

The sentences above are a way to remember the meaning of the terms *mean*, *median*, and *mode*. These measures, called **measures of central tendency,** are important when describing a set of data values.

When trying to remember the definitions of each of these terms, say the words out loud. Notice that *mode* actually sounds like the word *most*. The **mode** is the number that occurs *most* often in a set of data. In the set 3, 6, 7, 3, 8, the number 3 is the mode because it appears most often. A data set can have more than one mode or it can have no mode at all.

Median also sounds a lot like *medium,* which is a word that means "in the middle." The **median** is the number in the middle of the data set when the values are ordered from least to greatest. If there is an odd number of values in the set, the median is simply the value in the middle. If there is an even number of values in the set, average the two middle numbers.

If you use these similar-sounding keywords to remember the mode and the median, you can use process of elimination to remember what the mean measures. The **mean** of a data set is the average of the values. Remember that to average a data set, you find the sum of all of the values and then divide the sum by the number of values in the set.

When you come across objects in your everyday life that can remind you that the median is in the middle of a data set, point them out. For example, you may be trying on clothes in a store and you pull a size-medium sweater out of the middle of the rack. Or, you could be cruising along the highway admiring the newly planted flowers in the median strip, which is in the middle of the road. If you make these connections, you're sure to remember what the *median* of a data set represents!

Experiment with mnemonics...

Levels of Classification

▶ **K**ids **P**laying **C**heckers **O**n **F**reeways **G**et **S**quashed

In the 1700s, a scientist named Carolus Linnaeus came up with a way to classify living organisms. The system has seven levels, which are **kingdom, phylum, class, order, family, genus,** and **species.** Kingdom is the broadest category—think about the plant kingdom or the animal kingdom—and species is the most specific.

Organisms that are in the same category share certain characteristics. For example, any animal that belongs to the mammal class has fur or hair. Humans are sometimes called "homo sapiens"— that is because we belong to the genus *homo* and the species *sapiens.* The two young *homo sapiens* in the picture above look like they might be in trouble!

. . . .
It's Your Turn

Many people learn best by writing information over and over. Write the words *kingdom, phylum, class, order, family, genus,* and *species,* in order, ten times on a sheet of loose-leaf. Some of the words are difficult, so pay attention to the way they are spelled as you write them out. Then, fold the paper and see if you can recite the list from memory.

Types of Vertebrates

▶ **F**ive **b**lind **r**attlesnakes **m**odel **a**fros.

This acrostic can help you remember the five types of vertebrates. **Vertebrates** are animals that have a backbone. Humans, tree frogs, cobras, bass, crows, and dogs are examples of vertebrates. All other animals (without backbones) are invertebrates. Jellyfish, slugs, squid, bees, and butterflies are examples of invertebrates. Surprisingly, there are actually many more species of invertebrates than vertebrates. The first letter in each word of the acrostic stands for one of the groups of vertebrates.

The five groups of vertebrates are **fish, birds, reptiles, mammals,** and **amphibians.**

This acrostic is helpful for several reasons. The word *five* is part of the acrostic, and helps you remember that there are five groups of vertebrates. Also, the rattlesnakes in the acrostic are a type of vertebrate. In addition, the order of the words is important. There are more species of fish than there are species of birds. The acrostic lists the groups of vertebrates in order, based on how many species of each group there are.

If you are having trouble remembering what each word in the acrostic stands for, try to recite the word in the acrostic along with the group it represents. For example, say to yourself, "Five fish, blind birds, rattlesnakes reptiles, model mammals, afros amphibians."

The Basic Needs of Animals

▶ My mom was just wasting **oxygen** when she told us to **protect** ourselves from cramps by waiting an hour after eating **food** before going into the **water**. We couldn't wait!

This chaining mnemonic provides you with a list of the **four basic needs of animals.** Each highlighted word stands for a different need that all animals share.

All animals need to breathe, and all the animals on the earth breathe **oxygen.**

Another crucial need of all animals is **water.** Some animals, such as camels, can travel hundreds of miles before drinking water. Fish, on the other hand, cannot survive more than a minute outside of water. Still, both animals need water to survive.

The same can be said for **food.** Although food can come in many different forms, every animal needs food for energy.

Finally, some form of defense or **protection** is a basic need of all animals. Turtles have shells and cats have claws. These are both forms of protection.

Keep in mind that some animals may have more needs than these. For example, some animals need warm or cool environments in order to survive. But these four basic needs are common to all animals.

To help you remember this mnemonic, draw or imagine a picture that represents the sentence. Your picture should focus on the four highlighted words in the mnemonic. For example, you could draw a family that has just finished a picnic lunch near a river. You might want to draw some plates with scraps of food on them. The mother should be standing and talking to her children. Draw a big air bubble coming out of the mother's mouth to represent oxygen. She could be pointing to her stomach, or to a watch, indicating how her children need to protect themselves by waiting for their food to digest before getting into the water.

Commensalism

▶ "Come in, selfish men."

Symbiosis is a relationship between two organisms. In symbiotic relationships, four different things can happen. Sometimes, both creatures benefit (+, +). Sometimes, one creature benefits and the other is hurt (+, –). Sometimes, one creature is hurt and the other is not affected (–, 0). Occasionally, one creature benefits and the other is not affected (+, 0). This last example is known as commensalism.

The keywords help you understand the definition of commensalism. **Commensalism** is a symbiotic relationship between two different organisms in which one creature takes advantage and gains all the benefits. The other creature in this relationship does not gain anything, but it also is not hurt in any way—it is unaffected.

Examples:

- The remora, a bony fish, suctions onto a shark. The remora picks up scraps of the shark's leftover food without harming the shark.

- Orchids grow on trees, as close to the canopy as possible, where they can get better access to sunlight.

- The seeds of plants attach themselves to the fur of mobile vertebrates and thus get dispersed. The vertebrates don't seem to notice.

- Barnacles attach themselves to whales, scallops, and just about anything else. The barnacles get a place to live and the host is not bothered.

Keep in mind that you have to pronounce the keywords just right to help you remember. Practice pronouncing the keywords until you can make them sound almost exactly the same as the word *commensalism*. The "selfish men" are, of course, the organisms that benefit. Also, because you are playing the organism that is not helped or hurt in the relationship, try to use a dull, indifferent tone when you say, "Come in, selfish men."

Structural Organization

There are five increasingly complex **levels of structural organization** in organisms: cells, tissues, organs, organ systems, and organisms. You can use the pegword mnemonic to help you remember the levels of structural organization, in order, from the most basic to the most complex.

▶ The first level (remember one rhymes with bun) is the **cell** level. In this mnemonic, the bun is in a jail cell to help you remember that the first level of organization is the cell.

The second level (remember *two* rhymes with *shoe*) is the **tissue** level. There is toilet *tissue* stuck to the shoe in the picture.

The third level (remember *three* rhymes with *tree*) is the **organ** level. The musical *organs* in the picture can help you remember the body's organs.

The fourth level (remember *four* rhymes with *door*) is the **organ systems** level. The digestive system, one organ system in the body, is shown inside the door.

The fifth level (remember *five* rhymes with *hive*) is the **organism** level. Each bee in the picture is an organism.

Draw an alternative picture for the first level of structural organization of an organism. Remember, the picture should include a bun (for *one*) and something that clearly represents a *cell*. For example, maybe you talk on your *cell* phone all the time and you want to work that into the picture. You can come up with alternative pictures for the other levels, too, if you can think of more memorable images.

Homeostasis

There is no place like **home**ostasis!

Homeostasis is the biological process by which an organism resists change in order to maintain a stable condition. For example, your body reacts to changes in temperature by reacting to restore balance. If the weather is hot, you may perspire in an attempt to cool down. If the weather is cold, you may shiver or tremble in an attempt to create bodily heat. These regulatory measures are examples of homeostasis.

In the classic film *The Wizard of Oz,* Dorothy clicks her heels and repeats "There's no place like home." The changes in her environment have proven dangerous and terrifying, and she is hoping that her chant will restore her life to the way it was. Returning home brings the safety and stability that Dorothy needs. This desire for *home* is a good metaphor for homeostasis.

Your body's homeostatic systems work without your even having to think about it. However, think about things you consciously do to regulate your bodily comfort level. The next time you act on one of those processes—drinking water when you're thirsty or putting on a sweater when it's cold, for example—say to yourself "There's no place like homeostasis, there's no place like homeostasis." You can even click your heels if you want!

Arteries and Veins

▶ **A**rteries carry **A**way,
Veins carry **in**.

Arteries and veins are the major "carrying tubes" in blood circulation.

The **arteries** carry oxygen-rich blood away from the heart to the rest of the body. There, the oxygen and nutrients from the blood are absorbed by the muscles and other tissues. The aorta, which connects to the left ventricle of the heart, is the largest artery in the body. You can remember that *arteries* carry blood *away* from the heart because both words start with the letter *a*.

After the body's tissues have absorbed the oxygen, **veins** carry the "used" blood back to the heart. Veins have valves so that gravity does not cause blood to flow back down. A major vein is the pulmonary vein, which carries blood from the lungs to the heart. You can remember that veins go back into the heart because the word *in* is part of the word *vein*.

Use two fingers to find your pulse in your wrist or neck. As you feel the rhythm of your heart beating, close your eyes. Imagine that each time your heart beats, blood is being pumped into your arteries, which expand and then contract. That's why you can feel the throbbing. Repeat the line "Ar-ter-ies car-ry a-way" to the rhythm of your heartbeat.

Blood Types

Do you know your blood type? The four different types of blood are A, B, AB, and O. The letters *A* and *B* stand for two proteins that can be found in red blood cells. If your blood type is AB, then your blood has both proteins, and if your blood is Type O, it has neither protein. The most common blood type in the general population is Type O positive. ("Positive" refers to the presence of another antigen in the blood.) The rarest type is Type AB negative, which occurs in just 1 percent of the population.

Sometimes people get sick or injured, and they need a blood transfusion. However, it is dangerous for a person to receive blood if the type doesn't match his or her own. This could even lead to a fatal reaction. That is why it is important to know these rules: Type O blood can be given to anyone; that's why someone with Type O blood is known as a "universal donor." People with Type AB blood can receive any type of blood; that's why someone with Type AB blood is known as a "universal recipient."

Remember these important rules using the following mnemonic.

❝ *Get This . . .*

Students who are learning to read and play music have to memorize a lot of information, and acrostics are a popular tool for helping them. For example, the sentence "Every good boy does fine" has been used for years to help music students remember the notes on the lines of the treble clef. As you can tell from the sentence, the order of the notes from bottom to top is E, G, B, D, and F. The notes on the spaces of the treble clef can be remembered using the acronym FACE. ❞

▶ Type **O** is the universal d**O**nor.
Type **AB** can receive **A**ll **B**lood.

The Humerus

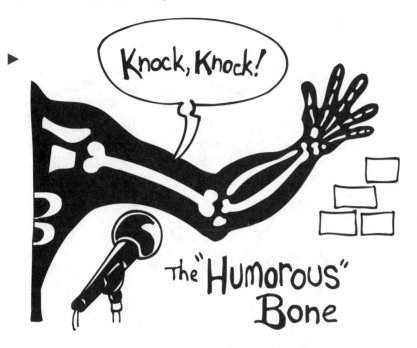

The **humerus** is the long bone in a human's upper arm. This bone starts at the shoulder and ends at the elbow.

A good way to recall the name of the humerus bone is to remember that it ends at the elbow, which is sometimes called the *"funny* bone." If you use the keyword *humorous,* which is a synonym for *funny,* you're sure to make the connection. You could even remember the upper arm's attempt at humor in the picture above to recall the name of the humerus bone.

It's Your Turn

Some people use keywords to help them learn a foreign language. Look at how we can use English keywords to remember Spanish vocabulary.

Lobo means "wolf." The keyword is *lobe,* so picture a wolf with pierced ears.

Oro means "gold." The keyword is *oar,* so picture a canoe with oars made of pure gold.

Pies means "feet." The keyword is *pie,* so picture someone squishing a bare foot into a pie.

Write the Spanish words on index cards and ask someone to test you. See if you can remember the English translations using mental pictures.

Bone Joints

▶

A joint is where two or more bones come together. The body has different types of joints so that we can move our parts in different directions.

One type of joint is the **ball-and-socket joint.** Your shoulders and hips are ball-and-socket joints because they can rotate in all directions. The big *ball* of yarn connected to the *sock* the old woman is knitting should help you remember ball and socket.

A second type of joint is the **hinge joint.** Your elbows and knees are hinge joints because they allow only back-and-forth movement. The screen door that is practically falling off its squeaky *hinges* will help you remember the hinge joint.

The third major type of joint is the **gliding joint.** Your wrist is a gliding joint, which is why you can move your hand from side to side and up and down. You can remember that the old woman in the picture is rocking back and forth in her *glider*.

Recruit a friend or family member to play a unique version of Simon Says with you. The person playing Simon should command the other player to make an action using one of the three types of bone joints. For example, Simon could say, "Simon says, 'Pretend to kick a soccer ball using a hinge joint,'" and the other player would pretend to kick a ball by bending his leg at the knee. The player should repeat this motion until Simon says to stop. As in any other game of Simon Says, the person receiving the commands should not follow the order unless it's preceded by "Simon says." When that person flubs, it's time to switch places.

Parts of the Ear

The ear is a complex body part. What we can see of the human ear is merely the outer ear. There are many small and fragile parts located inside the ear. The hole we can see in a human ear is the **auditory canal,** which travels from the outer ear to the middle ear. Sounds travel through the **eardrum,** causing tiny bones in the ear to vibrate. These bones are the **hammer, stirrup,** and **anvil.** Just above these bones are the **semicircular canals,** which aid in balance. In the inner ear are the **cochlea** and the **auditory nerve,** which transform vibrations into information. This information is then sent to the brain as sounds.

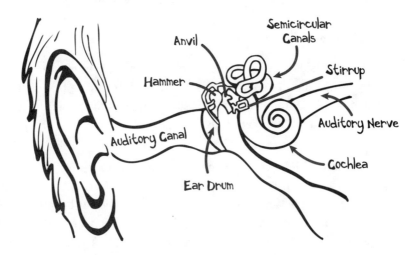

▶ You can help yourself remember the eight main parts of the human ear by chunking the information into categories.

Parts named after tools and instruments:	Parts involving canals:	Parts located at the back of the inner ear:
• eardrum	• auditory canal	• cochlea
• hammer	• semicircular canals	• auditory nerve
• stirrup		
• anvil		

Hearing Loss

▶ If you wanna keep hearing plenty,
Keep the sound below 120.

Do you turn the volume all the way up when you listen to your head-phones? Do you crank your favorite song when it comes on in the car, or have dance parties with music so loud that you and your friends have to shout to hear each other speak? Although there's nothing wrong with rocking out to your favorite song now and then, regularly listening to excessively loud music could cause long-term damage to your hearing.

We use units called **decibels** to measure the loudness of sounds. To give you a sense of scale, a whisper is about 20 decibels and a clap of thunder is about 110 decibels. If you turn your headphones up as loud as possible, the loudness of the music will probably be around 115 decibels. If you listen to music at 120 decibels or above—think of a live rock concert—you could definitely be causing damage to your ears. In fact, humans may actually feel pain when they hear sounds of 120 decibels and above; that pain is your body's self-protective way of saying, "Turn it down!"

The rhyme above can help you remember that 120 decibels is the pain threshold for sound for most people. You should keep your music at a level *well below* 120 decibels.

· · · · · · · · · · · ·
IT'S YOUR TURN

Have you ever heard the term *selective memory*? Our brains are good at filtering out unneeded information. For instance, if you need a penny, you just reach for the coin that's shiny copper and a bit smaller than a nickel—you don't need to memorize every feature of a penny. As a test, look at the following pictures. Can you identify which one is a *real* penny?

Xylem and Phloem

▶ **Xylem** zips water up,
Phloem floods food back down.

Vascular plants have vessels, or tubes, that carry water and nutrients to all parts of the plant. **Xylem** is the pathway that carries the water absorbed into the roots through the stem to the leaves. Then, photosynthesis takes place in the green leaves, creating sugar that plants use for energy.

Phloem is the pathway that carries the food from the leaves back to the roots, for storage, and to other parts of the plant, which use the energy. You can almost imagine that xylem and phloem make up a two-way street that runs between the roots and leaves.

The word *xylem* is pronounced "zī-lem." The repeated consonant sounds in the mnemonic—"*xylem zips*" and "*phloem floods*"—should help you remember the direction of each pathway. (See page 74 to learn more about repeating consonant sounds, or *alliteration*.)

. . . .
IT'S YOUR TURN

Most people's earliest childhood memories are from between the ages of 3 and 4. What is your earliest childhood memory? Can you recall any details about this experience, or is it just a vague image or a sensation that you remember? Once you pull up this early memory, run it by a sibling, parent, or anyone who was there at the time and see if they can confirm it. Of course, the photographs we see and the stories we hear from a young age influence our memories, so it's hard to know what is a "pure" memory.

Layers of the Earth

The earth is composed of layers. The three main layers are the crust, the mantle, and the core. The outermost layer of the earth is called the **crust;** this is the thinnest layer, with an average thickness of about 20 miles. The layer right under the crust is called the **mantle.** The center of the earth is known as the **core,** which is made up mostly of liquid and solid iron. The core is extremely hot—around 10,000 degrees Fahrenheit! Each layer has different chemical and physical properties that work together to create a balance of pressures and temperatures.

▶ Write the words *crust, mantle,* and *core* on index cards, which you will place around your bedroom.
- Put the card representing the **crust** on the wall.
- Put the card for **mantle** on the floor between the wall and the bed.
- Put the card for the **core** on the middle of your bed.

Using this mnemonic, you can remember that the crust is the outer layer of the earth (just like the wall is the outer layer of your room), the mantle is the in-between layer, and the core is the center.

Cut an apple in half. Look at the skin and notice how thin it is compared to the insides of the apple. Imagine that the skin is like the crust of the earth. The white fruit of the apple is similar to the mantle. And the solid, dense core at the center of the apple is like the core of the earth. Use this metaphor to help you remember the structure of the earth.

The Planets

▶ **My** **v**ery **e**nergetic **m**other **j**ust **s**erved **us** **n**ine **p**izzas.

*This acrostic tells you th*e order of the planets, starting with the planet closest to the Sun. The first letter in each word of the acrostic sentence is the first letter in the name of a planet. The letter *m* in *my* stands for Mercury, the *v* in *very* stands for Venus, and so on. The closest planet to the Sun is Mercury. So, the order of the planets is **Mercury, Venus, Earth, Mars, Jupiter, Saturn, Uranus, Neptune,** and **Pluto.**

Also, the acrostic mentions nine pizzas. This can help you remember that there are nine planets!

Write each word from the acrostic sentence on the front of an index card. On the back of each index card, write the name of the planet represented by that word. Line up the cards on the table to write out the acrostic. Choose a word, like *nine,* and see if you can remember which planet it stands for. Flip over the card to check your answer. Do this until you have flipped over all the cards.

. . . .
IT'S YOUR TURN

Come up with your own acrostic to help you remember the order of the planets. Choose one word from each list.

1. Many
   Mysterious
   Mister
   My

2. victorious
   vile
   vain
   very

3. eager
   electric
   evil
   experiment

4. mascot
   milkshake
   made
   museums

5. joyfully
   just
   jokes
   juveniles

6. swallowed
   sang
   sometimes
   silly

7. up
   unfortunate
   uncontrollable
   under

8. newspaper
   near
   nervous
   night

9. people.
   painfully.
   peacocks.
   pages.

The Layers of the Atmosphere

▶ My sister and I needed supplies for a camping trip. As we walked into the sporting goods store, there were **trop**ical plants on either side of the entrance. Straight ahead, near the escalators, was a map of the store. We used the map to plan our **strat**egy. Then, we went to the camping gear department on the second floor to find some **mes**h netting to keep bugs away and some **therm**oses to hold water. "Bugs and water, under control!" my sister declared.

There are four layers of Earth's atmosphere. The first layer of the atmosphere is the troposphere. The **troposphere** starts where the sea or the land ends. The air we breathe, and the air most airplanes travel in, is all part of the troposphere. Most of Earth's weather also takes place in the troposphere.

Some jets are capable of flying in the space above the troposphere. This area is called the **stratosphere.** Each layer of the atmosphere as you go higher up has thinner air. The temperature also increases with each layer.

The third layer of Earth's atmosphere is called the **mesosphere.** In this layer, shooting stars start to burn up.

The outermost layer of the atmosphere is the **thermosphere.** The air in this layer gets thinner and thinner until it eventually becomes outer space.

Notice that the highlighted word parts in the mnemonic do not provide the entire names of the layers of the atmospheres. This should not discourage you. Each layer of the atmosphere ends in the same seven letters, _–osphere_. If you can remember the key points of the loci method, you only need to add _–osphere_ to the end of each highlighted part.

The Hubble Space Telescope

▶ The "**Bubble**" Space Telescope

You may have heard of the **Hubble Space Telescope.** It is a very powerful optical telescope. The Hubble Space Telescope has been used to get extremely clear pictures of distant planets and galaxies. Before telescopes like the Hubble, it was difficult to obtain such clear pictures. This is because telescopes often receive images that are somewhat distorted and unclear. Earth's atmosphere causes these distortions, by blocking some types of light and energy. This is why the Hubble Space Telescope was such an important new technology. Earth's atmosphere does not affect the images received by the Hubble Space Telescope. Any idea why?

It is because the Hubble Space Telescope is not located on Earth. It floats in space, orbiting Earth. The keyword *bubble* can help you remember that the Hubble Space Telescope floats on the outer edge of Earth's atmosphere. Imagine that Earth's atmosphere is a bubble surrounding the planet. The Hubble Space Telescope floats around as if skimming the edge of this bubble around Earth.

Turn your head into a planet! Take a large plastic fishbowl, or other clear container. Try to look at several different objects through this container. Look at objects close up, like the words in a book, or objects that are farther away, like the house down the street. Take note of how these objects look through your homemade atmosphere. Can you see everything as clearly as if you did not have an atmosphere between your head and what you're viewing?

The Waxing and Waning Moon

▶ A big man's stomach when he is relaxing
is full and round, like the moon when it's waxing.
Now, think of your sink when the water is draining;
the water gets smaller, just like the moon waning.

This rhyming mnemonic can help you remember the meaning of the terms *waxing* and *waning*. You have probably noticed that the moon appears to get bigger or smaller in the sky. Each night, the amount of sunlight we can see reflecting off the moon is what makes the moon appear bigger or smaller. This occurs in phases. For the first half of the month, the moon starts as a small sliver and seems to get bigger each night. While the moon is getting bigger, it is said to be **waxing.** For the second half of the month, the moon starts as a full round moon, and then shrinks each night. This process is called **waning.**

Before you go to bed tonight, peer out your window or go outside and take a look at the moon. Even though you won't see the moon getting bigger or smaller, of course, you can tell whether the moon is waxing or waning on any given night. If the left side of the moon is dark and the right side is bright, that means the moon is waxing, or getting bigger. If the left side of the moon is bright and the right side is dark, that means the moon is waning, or getting smaller. You may need another mnemonic to remember that!

Properties of Waves

Waves have different properties. The **crest** of a wave is the highest point of a wave. It is the maximum distance upward from the rest position. The **trough** of a wave is the lowest point of a wave. It is the maximum distance downward from the rest position. The **wavelength** is the distance between successive crests or successive troughs. **Frequency** describes the number of wavelengths occurring in a given unit of time. **Amplitude** usually describes the height of a wave, or the distance from the rest position to the crest or the trough.

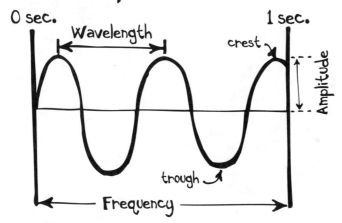

The Properties of Waves

0 sec.

1 sec.

Wavelength

crest

Amplitude

trough

Frequency

▶ Write the words *crest, trough, wavelength, frequency,* and *amplitude* on index cards. Then, walk around your home and put the cards in places where they can help you remember the meaning of the property.

First, tape the **crest** card to your bedroom ceiling because that is the highest point in your room. Next, place the **trough** card on the floor, the lowest point in the room. Put the **wavelength** card near a ruler because you use a ruler to measure distance. Then, place the **frequency** card near a calendar because a calendar represents time. Finally, put the **amplitude** card on the bed because that is where you take a rest.

The Electromagnetic Spectrum

Not all waves of light can be seen. In fact, as humans, we can see only a very small portion of all the radiation in the universe. But there is a wide range of different types of light in the universe. All these different wavelengths make up a scale called the **electromagnetic spectrum.**

▶ **Radio waves** have the longest wavelength. They are used in sending television and cell phone signals. Think about the hamburger bun (which rhymes with one) stuck on the antenna of a radio to remember that radio waves are first, or longest.

Microwaves are the next longest. Microwave ovens emit radiation that reheats your food. Picture a shoe (which rhymes with *two*) sitting in a microwave oven.

Next is **infrared** radiation. Remember the tall redwood tree (which rhymes with *three*) for infrared.

You're very familiar with the fourth type of light, **visible light**, which is near the middle of the spectrum. The sun and stars generally give off this kind of light. Picture door (which rhymes with *four*) with a window shaped like an eye to remember visible light.

Ultraviolet light has wavelengths that are just shorter than those of visible light. The atmosphere absorbs most of the sun's UV radiation, but some of it gets through and causes sunburn. Imagine a violet sticking out of a beehive (which rhymes with *five*).

As you probably know, **X-rays** are used for seeing through some substances. Remember the X-ray of the drummer holding up his sticks, which rhymes with *six!*

The shortest waves are called **gamma rays**. Picture a grandma, or "gamma," resting in heaven, which rhymes with *seven*.

Think about the color spectrum of visible light. It's just the colors of the rainbow: red, orange, yellow, green, blue, indigo, violet. (You probably learned another mnemonic, ROY G. BIV, to remember this!) Red has the longest wavelength, and violet has the shortest wavelength. This can help you remember that infrared is just beyond the longest range (red) of visible light and ultraviolet is just a little shorter than the shortest range (violet) of visible light. This way, you'll at least remember the middle part of the spectrum: infrared, visible, ultraviolet.

Types of Seismic Waves

▶ **S** waves bounce up and down, you see.
  Waves that go back and forth are called **P**.

Seismic waves are the shock waves produced by earthquakes. When the earth's crust suddenly shifts, vibrations are released and sent through the earth. The two major types of seismic waves are P waves and S waves.

Primary waves are better known as **P waves.** These are the fastest seismic waves. They travel in a back-and-forth motion through the rock, water, and liquid metal in the layers of the earth. P waves push and pull particles as they move through a substance. The motion of a P wave looks like a slinky that has been stretched taut and then quickly jerked.

On the other hand, **S waves,** or secondary waves, can travel only through solids. They travel in an up-and-down motion through rock particles, creating the second wave you feel in an earthquake. You can remember that an S wave looks like a curvy line, almost like the letter *S* turned on its side. Picture a jump rope that has been jerked downward.

When repeating the first line of the mnemonic, bounce up and down slowly, like you're doing squats. For the second line, shake your body back and forth as quickly as you can. Performing the movements along with the rhyme can help you remember the information, not to mention give you a good workout!

The Water Cycle

► **Ever try coconut pizza? Gross!**

This acrostic can help you remember the names of the different processes of the water cycle. The **water cycle** is how water travels throughout the earth's different ecosystems. Water is recycled and reused throughout the planet. The processes of the water cycle are all connected, and they keep repeating themselves so that earth is constantly getting a new supply of water. The highlighted letters in the acrostic stand for the five steps of the water cycle.

In the water cycle, water is absorbed into the air, where it becomes water vapor. Oceans and other bodies of water release water vapor through **evaporation.** Plants release water vapor into the air in a process called **transpiration.** The water vapor in the air then **condenses** to become clouds of water. The clouds eventually release this water back to Earth in a process called **precipitation,** which is also known as rain (or sleet or snow). Some of the falling water seeps into the ground. This **groundwater** eventually gets absorbed back into the roots of plants and drains into bodies of water. Then, the water cycle begins all over again!

Repeat the acrostic to yourself a few times until you can remember it without having to read it. To reinforce the mnemonic, you may want to think of how you would react if you tasted a slice of coconut pizza. You'd probably exclaim "Gross!" just as soon as you were able to grab a glass of water and wash the taste out of your mouth. Write down the first letter of each word in the acrostic, and then try to see how many water cycle processes you can remember. If you need extra incentive, imagine that for every process you forget, you will have to eat another bite of coconut pizza!

The Five Rock Cycle Processes

▶ That crazy **weather**man said the temperature would **cool** down this week, but by Saturday, the **heat** was so intense that we could **melt** a candy bar on the **cement** in seven minutes!

Rocks are formed from other rocks. The different factors in a rock's environment, such as heat, rain, or cold, cause one type of rock to change into another type of rock. In a way, rocks are constantly transforming into other types of rock. This is known as the **rock cycle.** There are five different processes in the rock cycle. The highlighted words in the chaining mnemonic represent these five processes. Each process results in a different type of rock being formed.

Below is a list of the five processes in the rock cycle and the type of rock each produces.

1. **Weathering** turns rocks into small particles called sediment.

2. **Cooling** turns hot magma into igneous rock.

3. **Heat,** combined with pressure, changes rocks into metamorphic rock.

4. **Melting** turns rocks into magma.

5. **Cementation** is a process where particles of sediment are glued together to form sedimentary rock.

You can draw a cartoon to help you remember this mnemonic. The first panel should show a weatherman at a desk labeled "weather." He could be holding a thermometer and pointing down, or perhaps pointing to a map that shows a cold front on the way. In the next panel of your cartoon, show some kids standing around watching a candy bar melt on the sidewalk. Maybe they're all bundled up in winter clothes as if they've listened to the inaccurate weather report. The kids could be sweating and there may be a thermometer that shows the mercury at 100 degrees. Make sure the five words *heat, weather, cool, cement,* and *melt* are included in your cartoon. Then, show a family member how this cartoon helps you remember the five rock cycle processes.

Pumice

▶ "Pum**ICE**"

The characteristics of igneous rock are very much like the qualities of an ice cube. **Pumice** is a type of igneous rock formed during volcanoes. When lava gets foamy and then cools, it forms pumice. Pumice is light in color, light in weight, and full of bubbles. And just like ice, it also floats in water.

Because pumice is both lightweight and abrasive, it is sometimes used in tooth or furniture polishes and in exfoliating beauty products. Some people use pumice stones to smooth the bottoms of their feet. Pumice is also a main ingredient in the rough Lava© soap (pumice comes from volcanic rock, hence the name Lava) that many painters use to scrub their hands clean. The unusual properties of pumice make it very useful!

When you say the mnemonic, emphasize the second syllable: pum•*ice*. This pronunciation will help you remember the characteristics of this igneous rock.

IT'S YOUR TURN

Study the following list of words for one minute:

car

icicle

milk

necklace

barn

key

bear

spoon

scissors

violin

Now, on a separate sheet of paper, try to list all ten of the words *in order*.

Compare your list to the one above and see how accurately you remembered the order of the words. If you want to test yourself again, have a family member make up another list of ten words (mostly nouns). This time, try a memorization technique. For example, create a story that involves all of the words in order, or try to imagine each object in a specific place in your bedroom.

Converting between Fahrenheit and Celsius

▶ Frank **equated** a **9–5** career **with 32** years of imprisonment.

You're probably familiar with both the Fahrenheit scale and the Celsius scale for measuring temperature. The Fahrenheit scale is widely used in the United States. In Fahrenheit, the freezing point of water is 32 degrees, the boiling point of water is 212 degrees, and normal body temperature is 98.6 degrees.

Most of the world uses the Celsius scale to measure temperature. In Celsius, the freezing point of water is 0 degrees, the boiling point of water is 100 degrees, and normal body temperature is 37 degrees.

Imagine you were visiting Italy and the morning news showed that the day's high temperature would be 20 degrees. Would you bring a sweater to go out sightseeing? In order to make this decision, you would need to be able to convert between Fahrenheit and Celsius. To convert between the two scales, we use the formula $F = \frac{9}{5}C + 32$.

❝ Get This . . .
Do you know what temperature is represented by the same number in both the Celsius scale and the Fahrenheit scale? The answer is –40 degrees. In other words, –40 degrees Celsius is the exact same temperature as –40 degrees Fahrenheit. To verify this fact, try plugging in –40 for C in the equation and solve for F. What do you find? ❞

The mnemonic sentence above is like a code to help you remember the formula. The F in *Frank* stands for Fahrenheit, the word *equated* stands for the equal sign, and "9–5" represents the fraction $\frac{9}{5}$. The C in *career* is for Celsius, and *with 32* reminds you to add the number 32. (People use 9–5 to mean 9 a.m. to 5 p.m., which is a standard full-time workday.)

Atmospheric Gases

There are a number of gases in Earth's atmosphere that make up what we call **air.** The main gases are nitrogen and oxygen. Nitrogen makes up about 78 percent of the volume of air and oxygen makes up about 21 percent. The symbol for **nitrogen** is N and the symbol for **oxygen** is O, so the word *NO* in the comic can help you remember these two main gases.

The remaining 1 percent of the air is made up of small amounts of other gases. These include **carbon dioxide** (CO_2) and **argon** (Ar). The words *see, oh,* and *two* will help you remember CO_2 and the phrase *are gone* will remind you of argon.

With the book closed, try to roughly sketch out the comic on a sheet of paper. See if you can recall the dialogue word for word, and underline the keywords that can help you remember the gases in air. Then, around the boys' heads, draw the symbols for the four main gases that make up the air. Make it look like the symbols are floating around the room.

Parts of an Atom

▶ PEN

The acronym PEN can help you remember the parts of an atom. An atom is the smallest part of a substance that still has all the properties of that substance. There are three different parts of an atom. The nucleus, or center, of an atom is made up of a cluster of **protons** and **neutrons.** Traveling around this cluster, like the Moon orbiting Earth, are **electrons.** Some atoms have hundreds of protons, neutrons, and electrons, while others have very few.

To give you some idea of just how small atoms really are, imagine a sandy beach. Try to imagine all the millions and millions of grains of sand that make up that beach. Now here's the hard part to imagine. There are as many atoms in one grain of sand as there are grains of sand on the entire beach! That's small!

. . . .
It's Your Turn

Sometimes, you know that there's an acronym to help you remember a certain set of information, but you can't remember what the acronym is. You may need to come up with a memorable way to remember the acronym PEN when you need to recall the parts of an atom. Because atoms are so unbelievably tiny, try this connection: How many atoms are there on the tip of a PEN?

Atomic Number of Oxygen

▶ "Octa-gen"

Let's take a trip down Memory Lane and review some basic chemistry. You may know that elements are made up of atoms, and that atoms contain particles called protons, neutrons, and electrons. We identify an element of the periodic table by how many protons it has. This value is known as the **atomic number** of an element. Because an atom has the same number of protons as it has electrons, the atomic number also tells us the number of electrons.

It is important to remember the atomic numbers of the common elements. The element oxygen (O) has an atomic number of 8 on the periodic table. That means an atom of oxygen has 8 protons and 8 electrons. The number of electrons is important because it helps us understand why oxygen forms chemical bonds with certain other elements.

The prefix *octa–* means eight. Think of an octagon, which has 8 sides, or an octopus, which has 8 tentacles. Use the keyword "octa-gen" to help you remember that the atomic number of oxygen is 8.

. . . .
IT'S YOUR TURN

Take out a sheet of paper. Now, try to list everything you ate for breakfast, lunch, and dinner for the past five days. It's more difficult than you thought it would be, isn't it?

Let's try something else. See if you can describe every outfit you've worn for the past five days. In the process of listing your outfits, did you remember anything else about what you had eaten? Sometimes remembering one specific thing can trigger another associated memory—especially if you dripped ketchup on your favorite white T-shirt on Tuesday!

Ionic Bonds

▶ "I own it" bonds

The process by which elements combine to form compounds is called **chemical bonding.** Examples of chemical bonds include sodium and chlorine combining to form table salt (NaCl) and hydrogen and oxygen combining to form water (H_2O). Atoms combine with other atoms by losing, gaining, or sharing electrons. Most atoms are stable when they have eight electrons in their outer energy level. Atoms combine with certain other atoms because they "seek" to become stable.

Table salt is formed through an ionic bond. Sodium has one electron in its outer shell and chlorine has seven electrons in its outer shell. So, chlorine has a very strong attraction to pull that one electron away from sodium to gain a stable outer energy level of eight electrons. Once that single electron is removed, sodium has a stable outer level too.

This kind of bond, which involves a *transfer* of electrons from one atom to another, is called an **ionic bond.** You can remember that in ionic bonds, one atom takes electrons from another atom using the keywords "I own it" bonds. Imagine a selfish chlorine atom snatching an electron from the sodium atom, declaring that it belongs to him now. Of course, the sodium atom is willing to part with a measly electron if it means he'll be stable too.

In **covalent bonds,** atoms *share* electrons so that their outer energy levels are stable. You can remember that covalent bonds involve sharing because of the prefix *co–*, which means "together with," as in *cooperate* or *coexist*.

Physical and Chemical Changes

▶ A shattered glass shouldn't make you feel quizzical;
the shards have just gone through a change that is physical.
A chemical change is more complicated;
it means a new substance has been created.

It can be tricky to figure out if an object has gone through a physical or a chemical change. This rhyming mnemonic can help you remember the difference between physical and chemical changes.

A **physical change** often involves a change in shape. A shattered glass looks very different from a whole glass, but all the molecules of the pieces are still the same. Many little pieces of glass are made up of the same elements as the whole glass. Even water that has been frozen into an ice cube has undergone a physical change. Cracking open an egg represents a physical change too. The shell that is in the garbage and the egg that is in the bowl, if put back together, would still have the same properties.

A **chemical change** involves a more permanent change in an object's properties. A chemical change usually involves a release of heat. An object that has gone through a chemical change is often turned into a new substance with new types of atoms. When a firecracker explodes, the paper and gunpowder are partly fused together. The burning releases energy, and some of the gas released is a new substance that was not present in the paper or the gunpowder alone.

Repeat the rhyming mnemonic out loud. Act like you are breaking a glass during the first part of the poem. During the second part of the poem, pretend you are building a campfire. When wood is burned, it releases certain gases and becomes a new substance, ash.

Density

▶ DenCity
Capitol Building

In social studies, a city has a higher population density than a rural town of the same size. That's because the people in the city area live closer together. In science, **density** describes the amount of matter in a given amount of space. In other words, density describes how tightly packed together the molecules in a substance are. For example, a metal spoon sinks to the bottom of a sink filled with water because the spoon is denser than the water.

The three types of matter are solids, liquids, and gases. Do you know which type of matter has the greatest density? **Solids,** such as glass and steel, are the densest type of matter. The next densest type of matter is **liquid,** and the least dense type of matter is **gas.** The picture on the previous page can help you remember this order if you think of each dot as a molecule. Notice that the dots in the air (gas) are very spread out. The dots showing the water (liquid) in the fountain are packed together a little more. And the dots in the stone wall (solid) surrounding the fountain and the capitol building itself are crammed together very tightly.

. . . .
IT'S YOUR TURN

Having a bad hair day? This may make it harder for people to recognize you. Studies have shown that hair is the most important feature for quick recognition. The color, density, and texture of the hair are cues that help us instantly identify people. Do a test. Find a fashion magazine and cut out the faces of eight well-known celebrities. Then, cut away their hair and "trade" their locks. For example, you might tape Carrot Top's curly red mane to Chris Rock's face! Then, flash each picture for two seconds and see if your friends can identify each celebrity face without his or her real hair. It's tougher than it sounds!

Newton's Laws of Motion

In 1687, Isaac Newton published a paper outlining the three basic laws of motion.

The **first law of motion** states that an object that is at rest will remain at rest unless something forces it to start moving. The flip side of this law is that an object in motion will continue moving in the same direction until some force, such as friction, causes it to slow or stop. The first picture will help you remember this law because the hamburger bun (which rhymes with *one*) is "at rest."

NEWTON'S 1ST LAW

An object at rest stays at rest,
and an object in motion stays in motion.

The **second law of motion** is a mathematical formula that states that force equals mass times acceleration. So, if the same force is applied to objects with different masses, the acceleration will be less for the object with the greater mass. This is illustrated by the second picture: The shoe (which rhymes with *two*) kicks the bowling ball (ouch!) and the soccer ball with the same force, but the bowling bowl moves more slowly because it has the greater mass.

NEWTON'S 2ND LAW

Force = Mass X Acceleration

The **third law of motion** talks about a force applied to an object. It states that when a force is applied, the same amount of force will push in the opposite direction too. This is illustrated by the third picture in which the kid wings the baseball at the tree (which rhymes with *three*), and it bounces off in the opposite direction, heading straight for his head. Unfortunately for him, the tree exerted the same force on the ball that the ball exerted on the tree!

For every action, there is an equal and opposite reaction.

Next time you watch a baseball game, be on the lookout for the third law of motion. For example, if a player's bat breaks, turn to the person next to you and explain that, because of Newton's Third Law of Motion, the baseball exerted as much of a force on the bat as the bat did on the baseball, thus causing the ball to ricochet onto the field and half of the bat to fly into the dugout. Then, be prepared to run when that person threatens to beat you up for talking about physics during the ball game!

Simple Machines

▶ I was pulling Lee's super wedgie.

This acrostic can help you remember the six simple machines that can be used to change the direction or size of a force. These six simple machines are an inclined plane, a wheel and axle, a pulley, a lever, a screw, and a wedge. The first letter in each word of the sentence is the first letter in the name of a simple machine.

The *I* stands for an **inclined plane.** An inclined plane is a flat surface like a smooth board. When the plane is inclined, or slanted, it can help you move objects. A common inclined plane is a ramp.

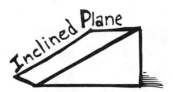

The *w* in *was* stands for a **wheel and axle,** a simple machine that moves objects across distances. The rotation of the wheel turns the axle, a cylinder-shaped post, causing movement.

The *p* in *pulling* stands for a **pulley,** a cord that wraps around a wheel. As the wheel rotates, the cord moves. Attach a hook to the cord, and you can use the pulley's rotation to raise and lower objects. The word *pulling* is similar to the word *pulley* too!

The *L* in *Lee's* stands for a **lever,** a tool that pries something loose. Think of a crowbar or the claw end of a hammer that you use to pry nails loose. (For more information on levers, see page 232.)

The *s* in *super* stands for a **screw,** an inclined plane wrapped around a cylinder. Every turn of a metal screw helps you move the metal through the wood.

The *w* in *wedgie* stands for a **wedge,** which can be used to push things apart or split them. An axe blade is a wedge. Think of the edge of the blade as two smooth slanted surfaces meeting at a point. The word *wedgie* is similar to the word *wedge* too!

Think of someone you know whose name begins with *L*—Larry, Lisa, Lee, Lana, anyone. Recite the mnemonic again, but replace Lee's name with your friend's name. Then, imagine you were giving your friend a super wedgie! (Don't actually do it, though, because that's mean!) Review the mnemonic again and visualize each simple tool with the first letter of each word.

The Lever

▶ **L**ifts
  Even
  Very
  Enormous
  Rhinos

This acronym icon reminds you of the abilities of a lever. **A lever** is a type of simple machine. Levers can help apply force to an object while using less effort. It can also change the direction of the force needed. For example, if you need to remove the top off a wooden box, you have to try and push up on the edge of the box. If you use a lever, such as a crowbar, you can insert an edge of your lever under the lid, then push down on your lever.

The three parts of a lever are the effort arm, the fulcrum, and the resistance arm. The effort arm is the part of the lever that you apply effort to. The fulcrum is like the middle of the lever, but is not always located in the center. The fulcrum is the point where the effort arm ends and the resistance arm begins. The resistance arm changes your effort into force against the object you are trying to move.

Basically, the longer the effort arm is, the less force you need to move a specific object. So, even though it would take a strong weight lifter to lift a 500-pound couch off the ground, a small child could lift the same couch if he had the right lever.

❝ Get This . . .

Acronyms are used to help you remember, but they're also used to shorten unwieldy phrases or titles. For example, the word *scuba* is actually an acronym that stands for "self-contained underwater breathing apparatus." And many people aren't aware, but the USA PATRIOT Act, which was passed after the terrorist attacks of 2001, is short for Uniting and Strengthening America by Providing Appropriate Tools Required to Intercept and Obstruct Terrorism. Can you imagine repeating that mouthful over and over on the Senate floor? ❞

Light Passing through Objects

▶ "trans-pair-of-glasses"
"trans-loose-leaf"
"o-peg"

In optics, objects are classified as transparent, translucent, or opaque based on how much light they allow to pass through them.

A **transparent** substance is one that allows all light to pass through. Images can be seen clearly through transparent materials, examples of which include plastic wrap and clear glass. You can remember the definition of *transparent* using the keyword "trans-pair-of-glasses" because the lenses in a pair of eyeglasses are an example of transparent material.

A **translucent** substance is one that allows some light to pass through. Examples of translucent materials include tissue paper, some plastic food containers, lightweight curtains, and mottled glass. The keyword "trans-loose-leaf" can help you remember the mean of *translucent* because a sheet of loose-leaf paper allows some light to pass through.

An **opaque** substance is one that allows no light to pass through. Examples of opaque materials include bricks, book jackets, aluminum foil, and leather. To remember the meaning of opaque, think of the keyword "o-peg" and imagine a wooden peg that allows no light to pass through it.

Go through all the stuff in your kitchen and put it into three piles. The first pile should include transparent objects, the second pile should include translucent materials, and the third pile should include opaque things. See if you can find at least four examples of each, and be sure to put everything back when you're finished!

Brock Microscope

When looking at very small objects in science class, you may use a **Brock microscope.** This is a sturdy and simple microscope with only one lens and one moving piece.

To remember the parts of a Brock microscope, visualize the scene from the stage play involving an old-time baseball player. Each labeled part of the scene stands for a part of the Brock microscope.

Remember that the Brock microscope has an **eyepiece** (note the eyepiece of the camera), an **arm** (note the player's extended arm), a **stage** (the drama is taking place on a stage), a **base** (the player is rounding first base), a **light source** (see the photographer's flashbulb), and a **lens** (note the camera lens).

❝ Get This . . .

Some people have even used the loci method to remember grocery lists. For example, if you need to remember to buy carrots, olive oil, and bread, you might picture a giant carrot lounging on your bed, slippery oil spilled in the hallway, and a loaf of bread wedged between the books on your bookshelf. These items are usually easier to remember if you can picture them in strange settings. **❞**

The Scientific Method

▶ **O**wls **h**ave **p**retty **t**ough **c**laws.

This acrostic can help you remember the steps of the **scientific method.** The scientific method is used by all scientists. It is a process for figuring out new laws of nature or proving that old laws might be incorrect.

This acrostic presents the five steps of the scientific method in order.

1. **Observation:** Observe certain trends that happen and make notes.

2. **Hypothesis:** Make an educated guess that you will attempt to prove.

3. **Prediction:** State what you believe your experiment will prove based on your observations.

4. **Test:** Conduct tests, or experiments, that attempt to prove your hypothesis.

. . . .
IT'S YOUR TURN

The scientific method is important for all scientists. The order of the steps represented by the acrostic must be followed as shown. You may want to create your own memorable acrostic to help you remember the scientific method. The five words in your sentence must start with the letters *O, H, P, T,* and *C.*

5. **Conclusion:** If the tests prove you right, your conclusion may be very similar to your hypothesis. If your tests do not support your hypothesis, your conclusion might explain why you got different results than expected.

In order to remember that this acrostic represents the steps of the scientific method, think of the sentence "Owls have pretty tough claws" as an *observation* a scientist might make in a study on owls.

Fighting Bacteria

Every year, more than 70 million people in the United States get food-borne illnesses, such as salmonella and E. coli. There are ways to prepare food safely and prevent illness by fighting bad bacteria. One of the obvious ways is to keep kitchen surfaces, such as countertops, clean. Foods that need cooling should be kept in the refrigerator. When cooking, make sure you use a high enough temperature to cook food thoroughly and kill bacteria. Finally, don't allow certain uncooked foods (or their juices) to mix when preparing them.

Take an imaginary walk around your kitchen. As you look at the refrigerator, the sink, the stove, and the counter, you can recall four ways to keep food safe from bacteria.

66 Get This . . .

The Greek poet Simonides of Ceos is said to have invented the loci method of memorization. The story goes that at a banquet, Simonides read a poem in honor of his host, but the poem also praised two Greek gods. The angry host told the poet that he would pay him only half of his fee. A bit later, Simonides left the banquet hall when a message was brought saying two men were waiting outside to see him. While he was gone, the roof fell in, crushing the guests and the self-centered host.

When the mangled bodies were uncovered, even their relatives couldn't tell who was who. But using a mental image of the order in which the guests had been seated around the table, Simonides was able to identify all the corpses, so the families could bury their dead.

The Greeks learned a meaningful lesson from this story: memory techniques —good, insulting the gods—bad! 99